The Traveller, Lost

The Traveller, Lost

Glenn Martin

G.P. Martin Publishing

Published 2025 by G.P. Martin Publishing

Website: www.glennmartin.com.au

Contact: info@glennmartin.com.au

Book layout and cover design by the author.

The sketch at the centre of the front cover is by Owyn Coetsee.

Typeset in Sitka 11 pt

Printed by Lulu.com

ISBN: 978 0 6459543 9 5 (pbk.)

NATIONAL LIBRARY OF AUSTRALIA

A catalogue record for this book is available from the National Library of Australia

The Handbook of Lu, the Wanderer

We are wanderers,
despite the effort to be anchored in plans.
We are chosen to be in moments
we are unprepared for,
just so we can learn to appreciate
that too, and that.

The wanderer learns not to presume,
not to depend on solidity
however solid it may seem.

We wander best
with simple rules:
To enjoy.
To act with correctness.
To be bold but polite.
To know stillness in movement.
It is grand.

Contents

.

Chapter 1: A trip to Britain and Ireland

The path through life can be described in many ways. One writer describes it as a beginning in obscurity, out of which we develop a sense of idealism. This results, one hopes, in the development of competencies which allow one to pursue the elements of our idealism. But ultimately, there is light, just light. It is effortless and all-consuming, although one might also say it is simply light radiating infinitely: everywhere, everywhere.

The obscurity is because we are starting out new, and everything is happening all around us: all of life, so many things. And who are we in the midst of this, and what are we to become? What are we to make of ourselves?

So, we start out, and we might hear useful things that help to guide us. When I was young, I joined the Boy Scouts, and they always said, "Be Prepared". It seemed like very sensible advice. Mind you, we remember many statements like this, and that in itself can be confusing. For the Boy Scouts the statement is bundled up with ethics and responsibility, social conventions and historical anachronisms. But I still like to think that being prepared was very useful advice.

The result is that we oscillate between two desires. One is to create a home in this unfamiliar, unstable and unpredictable world, and one where, for the most part, we are not in a position of control. We do not have that power. We seek to make a home and to make it safe and comfortable. But the other desire is to travel and adventure, for we know there is something integral about adventure in life. We cannot confine ourselves to the one place and the one set of rigid ways; we have to explore, and explore widely.

And so, travel is an essential aspect of our being.

However, not getting lost is an essential competency for the traveller, because, to be lost is to be fearful of the consequences if the situation does not resolve itself. Mythically, one can be lost forever, going round and round fruitlessly, wasting away, lost to one's kin and home, swallowed up by the wilderness, and prey to monsters. It is right that the surroundings are unfamiliar: after all, we are travelling, wandering, venturing, but when we are lost, nothing corresponds with the map or the directions we have been given, and nothing promising is eventuating.

In the early convict colony in Australia, convicts desperate to escape from the privations and brutality of the settlement went off into the bush, thinking that China lay only a few hundred miles to the north. Sometimes they wandered back into the prison colony a week later, hungrier and defeated. Sometimes their bones were found months or years later out in the bush.

Not getting lost was a competency I learned early in life, through the Boy Scouts. We learned to read a map, go walking in the bush, follow a route, and find our way to a destination. At that time, we were coming home to parents, and the adventure in the middle was to find a desirable place on the map: a mountain, a ridge, a peak, a river. And, to be at risk of getting lost. But we seldom had very much difficulty in completing our journey, although sometimes there were unsettling moments.

One time I was with two other scouts in the Snowy Mountains, on a three-day walk, and one afternoon the mist blew in. We could scarcely see twenty metres in front of us, in addition to which the track was altogether vague, not often trod. The terrain was hilly, with large granite boulders scattered among long grass. The white boulders in the mist were quite ghostly. It was an anxious two hours we had before we came upon the small mountain cabin for which we had been aiming.

Afterwards we would say we were not totally lost; it was just unsettling, a test of our nerve. For sixteen- and eighteen-year-olds it was a good test. It fed our feeling of accomplishment when we returned home.

It is beneficial to go somewhere; this is the way to test and prove our stillness and clarity.

I Ching, 22, Thomas Cleary

Many years later, as an undeniably older person, I went to England for a trip. Going to Scotland and Ireland were also part of the trip. There were family history reasons for these travels (I was on the trail of the ancestors), as well as the desire to see places I hadn't seen before, and to see beautiful places.

I prepared as well as I could. I spent hours pored over maps spread out on the floor, trying to imbibe the lay of the land, as well as choosing where I would go. I also looked at maps on-screen, digesting the relationships of towns to each other, towns to shorelines, and streets within townships. I did my best to learn what I was going to encounter, the shape of it, to Be Prepared.

I had been to Britain and Ireland once before, seven years previously, although this time I was going to see different places, except for London. I had been to London last time, but there was more to see. But I felt confident. And technology had come a long way in seven years. I had a mobile phone with Google Maps on it.

I was not going to hire a car, so my means of transport were buses and trains, and occasionally a plane. And I would walk. I had a sturdy pair of shoes for walking, and when I go to a new place, I like to put my feet on the ground. Walking is how I get the feel of a place. I could have even said at the outset, "What could go wrong?", but I didn't, because that would be to tempt the unwanted.

Accordingly, I did not expect to get lost, at least not deeply lost, lost-for-hours lost, frequently lost, and dizzyingly back-to-front, north-south and east-west lost. It seemed ridiculous, but more often than not, I was a traveller, lost.

I was not fearful. My ground had been mapped. If it was not familiar to me, it was familiar to many. They took it for granted. I assumed that I would make it so for myself, that I could step into this accomplished familiarity.

My trip was six weeks long. I started out in London. One doesn't start by thinking of trials. Reality tends to be practical: tickets purchased, accommodation organised, lists of destinations, arrangements, events and excursions planned. One applies the best of common sense: don't try to do too much, be satisfied with what is achievable, enjoy. Discover the new, appreciate it all. This is what it means to be prepared.

Yet some say there is a ring of trials that humans must experience. At the beginning, we come into this world and we forget who we were before the beginning. We were light radiating infinitely: everywhere. But we do forget. That is a condition of our passage. This is the first trial. We must muddle along, trying to figure it out: who are we? And then we discover the five senses, and we are distracted by them. We learn competencies but we find it hard to distinguish reality from illusion.

We go deeper and deeper. This is the second trial. It is long and often difficult, occasionally painful. It seems at times that we could be engulfed and lost forever. So what is the last trial, we ask? The last great trial is letting go. Can we travel through what the world presents us with and not be defeated: lost and defeated? Are our competencies sufficient to get us through successfully?

Why do we travel? Eric Newby (in *A Traveller's Life*, 1985) says there are various reasons. Some people travel to escape their creditors.

Others are seeking a warmer or a cooler clime. Some are out to sell Coca-Cola to the Chinese (this was in 1982). Others just want to find out what is over the hills and far away, over the seas, round the corner, or over the garden wall. Evelyn Waugh (who wrote the introduction to Newby's book) said it is to satisfy the romantic longing that lies deep in our hearts, and to do so it is necessary to shun the spectacles of the tourist.

The tourist is looking for escape; the traveller is looking for experience.

Chapter 2: A long way to London

To get to London from Sydney, one takes a plane. I don't know that anyone looks forward to the journey. It is a long way, and it is a long time, usually more than twenty-four hours. I have two thoughts that make the journey tolerable. The first is a mantra: "I am luggage, just luggage. The important thing is that I arrive undamaged." The second thought is that it would be churlish to complain about a journey to London that takes twenty-four hours when all my direct ancestors, coming from the British Isles to Australia, took from three to five months in a ship on seas that were often dangerously rough.

"I am luggage. My intention, insofar as I am capable of influencing the outcome, is to arrive safely." I tend to the practicalities: a modest imbibement of food and drink (non-alcoholic), toileting, sleep (as possible, even sitting up), and a modest amount of entertainment. On this trip to London, I didn't fare well with one aspect. I took a book to read, but my eyes are not what they used to be, and the light was not sufficient for me to read most of the time. That was a disappointment.

During the day part of the flight, from Doha to London, I was able to read, and most people around me were asleep, so it was quiet. Ironically, in the book I was reading, there was an episode where the character lost most of her sight, a condition which lasted for about three months. She was an artist, so she was also estranged from her usual work. The question that was raised for her was, do I still trust life?

Noted.

After this (in the book), there was a story about the lady coming back to London: she had grown up there, and she described a part of London where she and a friend went to school. Curious!

We got to London about 12:30 pm. I managed to go through all the steps to exit the airport without trial or mishap. I got to the train to go to the place where I was going to stay, and it went a long way around, but the route was simple for me. It only involved one change, from the tube to a train. The trains were crowded. It was Bank Holiday today, and people were out having fun. It was a festive air, happy and exuberant.

I made one mistake; I got off the train two stations early. There was a reason for that: I misread the number of stations, but it was okay. I simply waited for the next train. I walked up the road from the Herne Hill station, with my suitcase (which was not too big or heavy; I had made sacrifices) and my backpack, a few hundred metres, and found the house: two-stories, perhaps 100 years old. I was welcomed.

The first thing I heard in the morning was the call of doves, just as in Kate Bush's "Aerial" album. So, a familiar sound.

After breakfast I walked down to the station and caught a train into the city, to Victoria Station.

Your home is behind you; the world lies ahead.

Gandalf to Bilbo Baggins, in *The Hobbit*, J.R.R. Tolkien

Buckingham Palace was nearby, so I walked up the street towards it. It was starting to drizzle. When I got close, there were policemen, and some roads were closed to traffic. I got to a gateway into a walled park, and there was a queue of people inside, many with umbrellas. I heard that there was going to be a trooping of soldiers today, a rehearsal for some military parade.

I wasn't attracted to standing in the queue and waiting for a display of military might. I had seen the palace as an outsider from where I was standing, just as my ancestors would have seen it, ordinary people. I walked away, down towards Big Ben, past Westminster Abbey, which I had seen on my last trip. I saw Big Ben and the houses of parliament, and they were elaborate and beautiful.

I found myself near to the Tate Britain gallery, so I went in there to dry out from the rain. I looked at the exhibitions. One was of the International Association of Artists, from just before World War 2. There was the feeling that artists had to stand (internationally) against war, but it was a minor political association; it was not going to turn the tide of society.

I walked down the road. I was in Millbank, where a prison had been, where Sarah Crosby (my Irish great great grandmother) had been confined in 1849, after her trial and sentencing, before she was transported to Australia on the *St Vincent*. She had stabbed a policeman in the arm, in desperation after he had told her to get out of the Refuge for the Homeless Poor where she hoped to get a bed for the night in the middle of winter, and he had pushed her down on the ground and had his knee in her chest.

I had been to this place before, in 2018. There is nothing left of the prison, but I saw Henry Moore's sculpture on the riverbank commemorating the prison and all its unfortunate inmates.

I walked past the Oval, the cricket stadium. Even though it was wet and there was no match on, there were staff scurrying around, shifting boxes of goods. I walked for another 30-60 minutes. This area was a place of apartment blocks about three stories high, not a flash neighbourhood but functional, peaceful, not a disaster. I found a shop to have some lunch. One of my daughters had told me that when she lived in London, there were good sandwich shops all over. I found a shop, Pret a Manger, that had good sandwiches. It was enjoyable.

I studied Google Maps to try to head for something interesting. I decided that I was south of the main city, so I could walk back to Brixton. I set directions, and it kept telling me I was ten minutes away. I kept walking and I seemed to be progressing. However, after a while, I started to feel that I was not getting any closer. After twenty minutes, I was still ten minutes away. I wasn't even clear about north, south, east and west.

However, there were signs for the Elephant & Castle station, which I knew was near to where I was staying, at Herne Hill, so I tried for that. I thought it would be best to get a bus or train from here. I looked up directions to get to my destination by bus, but it turned out that I was heading in the wrong direction. When the (apparently) right bus turned up, I asked the driver. It confirmed what I had wondered about: I was in the right place but heading in exactly the wrong direction. He told me to stay on the bus until we got to the next bus stop, then get off and cross the road.

So, I changed buses, and this time I was heading south. I wasn't sure how I would tell how to get off. I figured it was about five suburbs. I had looked at this area on Google Maps two weeks ago, and I recognised the names of a few places. When we got to Denmark Hill I got off, because I knew I was now close. That was fine. I had to walk about a kilometre, but the rain had ceased for the afternoon, and I managed to get to my destination unproblematically.

We travel, initially, to lose ourselves; and we travel, next, to find ourselves.

Pico Iyer

I suppose that wasn't bad for a first day. The walking seems to be necessary to get my feet on the ground in the new country. People seem to have viable lives here; for the most part they seem to be functional and accepting of it. There is no overriding sense of desolation or desperation.

The next day I decided I should go to the British Library. It was a warm day. I turned out to be adept at finding my way, getting the train into the city, then alighting at the correct station and walking to the library, up streets where I had not been before.

The British Library is a newish building, with brown bricks to echo the railway station. When I got there, maybe 9:30 am, there was a long queue of people, mostly of school student age. I asked the young Indian lady in front of me why this was so. She said, very politely, that it was half-term break, and the students would have projects that required them to visit here. Anyway, the queue moved quickly.

Once I was inside, I thought I should see an exhibition. There was one about treasures held by the library. There were pages of notebooks from Leonardo da Vinci, sacred texts such as early Hindu books, along with Japanese books, the Declaration of the end of slavery in America, with the face of Abraham Lincoln and images from the 36 states that signed it. There was a copy of the Magna Carta, and handwritten pages by the Beatles: the lyrics for "In My Life" and a few other songs. There were also notes and letters by some famous writers.

9

There was nothing about the I Ching. I had finished writing a book on the I Ching this year, and I was curious about whether it is fading out of sight in society today. Looking for books on the I Ching in bookshops had become a point of curiosity for me.

To access books in the library, you have to register as a Reader. I didn't think it necessary for me to do that, but I asked about looking at the catalogue. It is, of course, online, so I sat and used my phone to go through the catalogue, searching for what they had on the I Ching. There were 2-3 thousand results, but we know that after the first 20-50 pages of results, the connections of entries to the I Ching would be rather loose. And so it was.

I looked at about 200 results, and it confirmed my impressions. The main books and writers that I have at home were present in the library: Legge, Wilhelm, Blofeld, Shaughnessy, Minford. I think they didn't have a few that I've got, such as Alfred Huang. But they had several of Stephen Karcher's books. In all, I counted about twenty books that I have.

I didn't stay for too long. I wanted to see some bookshops. One is called "Word on the Water" and it is on a barge in a canal north of St Pancras station. I took a wrong turn, but in doing so I found the St Pancras church. It is very old stonework, where the stones had rounded edges, looking rougher than modern stonework. It was in a lovely walled yard with trees. I went inside the church and there were chairs (old chairs) instead of pews. It felt rustic. The church was beautifully decorated.

I was sure someone in the family tree got married here. [Back at home, I checked in the family tree. There were no marriages, but three people were baptised there: John Bulling, in 1825 (son of James Bulling & Hannah Durnford), Emma Bulling, in 1827 (same parents), and Richard Lewis, 1840 (a younger brother of Edward Lewis!). Edward Lewis was the husband of Sarah Crosby. He was also a convict, and he was in a London orphanage when he was ten.]

I walked up the hill and over to the canal, walking along the canal now. I found the boat; the shop opened at 12 noon. It was quirky, with plants and old typewriters along the deck, out in the weather. Inside it had books, but it also had a couple of lounges. There were numerous customers, no doubt attracted by the description on the website, Bookshops of London. For a tiny bookshop, they had a good selection of up-to-date books, as well as some classics.

I did not buy anything. There were numerous books I could have bought, but I don't feel compelled at the moment. What am I going to read? What do I feel the need to read? My mind is brewing, and the brew is not clear yet.

> I am not going anywhere. I am only on the way. I am making a pilgrimage.
>
> *Siddhartha*, Herman Hesse

I walked down to Waterstones bookstore. The streets were crowded. Around St Pancras, there seemed to be lots of people who had just arrived in London (ah, the trains come in from Europe!). I walked past Chinatown and through Soho. I walked a long way, having not really mastered the navigator on the phone. I did get to Waterstones, five stories of it. I needed a drink and some food, but the café in the bookshop only had cakes, so I just had a drink.

The café was crowded, so I asked a man if I could sit at his table, a black gentleman who told me he was from the Sudan. Then there were two women who were also sitting at the table, the gentleman told me. They had gone to get tea. They returned with their tea and we all talked. The two ladies had been at school together, and the bookshop was a convenient place for them to meet. They both lived south of London. The man was well-spoken. He lived in the UK, but he had been born in Sudan, under British rule. He had worked in the

British embassy and had experienced what life was like under the British in the Sudan. He was reading a book called *The State of Us*.

We talked about things that strangers from different countries and backgrounds talk about. One of the ladies asked me what it was like in Australia, and if things had improved. She was referring to our recent election results, when Labor under Anthony Albanese had decisively defeated the Liberals under Scott Morrison. The lady was adamantly anti-Trump. I told her that people like me were comforted with the results. Australia had made a clear choice not to go down the pathway of Donald Trump. I described him as preposterous, and this struck a chord with them.

Then I looked through the books at the shop. It was a nice shop, and they had an interesting collection, very current. But although they had a large Philosophy section and Religion section, there was not one book on the I Ching. The question remains, is it dying out except for some people who like obscure things?

I walked again, and had a sandwich in a large park (Russell Square) which was like Centennial Park in Sydney, even down to the presence of horses as well as bicycles. I ended up at Bond Street Station, but I was stumped as to how to get to Herne Hill. I asked an attendant and he said to go to Canary Wharf and change. I thought this was wrong, and I recognised Farrington, which is where I changed on my first day, so I went there and changed to the overground going to Herne Hill.

It was near peak hour, so it was crowded. And then the train stopped because, we were told, there was a problem with signals. We stood there waiting for 10-15 minutes. I suppose I should be grateful there were announcements. I went the wrong way when I got out of the station. I am still having trouble orienting myself, although more things are familiar. I had my doubts quite soon, and corrected myself, walking back the other way and noting the signs.

She who is outside her door has the hardest part of her journey behind her.

Dutch proverb

Chapter 3: A visit to St Paul's

I was in London. I wanted to see some things that are probably worth seeing.

I went to St Paul's Cathedral, walking up from London Blackfriars station. It was crowded, but not too crowded. I bought the booklet as well as a ticket for a tour. The place is huge inside, and ornate: stained glass, stone columns, elaborate ceiling and many sculptures. The guide for the tour was Scottish. He thought my accent might be Antipodean; this apparently is the word used when people don't want to offend Australians or New Zealanders.

The guide's information was insightful. He recounted the history of the place, including the reasons for its foundation. I think he said this is the sixth church on the spot. The current one dates from rebuilding after the great fire of London in 1666. He talked about German bombs in World War 2. It was not hit by any explosive bombs, but there were also incendiary bombs which started fires. In the great fire of London, the lead melted off the roof in rivers. During the war, volunteer people stayed at the church at night to put out any fires on the roof started by the German bombs.

In the middle of all the frenetic tourist activity, a minister stood up at a pulpit to say prayers over the loudspeakers.

The most impressive statue was of Wellington, a great artifice with a prone body lying in the middle, amid horses and metaphorical scenes, such as a battle between truth and falsehood.

I went downstairs to the crypt where famous people are buried, and there are statues. There are a lot of famous people. Most of them are military and naval. Some are scientists or architects, such as Christopher Wren.

Then I went up to the dome. From the ground you can ascend stairways right up to the top of the cathedral. One level is the Whispering Gallery, where you walk around the base of the dome, and whispers can be heard across from one side to the other. Then you go up again, and it gets very narrow in some sections. I had to rest a couple of times. There are over 500 steps.

Eventually you come out onto a balcony that goes around the dome, and you can see all of London. You can walk all the way around, 360 degrees. It is so high that a little girl near me asked her father, "Are they toys down there?" He said, "No, they are people."

I walked all the way back down. It was a good test of my ability to accomplish it "at my age". When I got back down to the ground, a lady official gave me a soft applause. I went to the café in the basement and had a pumpkin scone, which was lovely.

I wanted to see Foyles bookstore. I found my way there, tentatively, with Google Maps.

They did have some books on the I Ching; in fact they had what I considered to be a good selection for a shop. I got a photo of one, to buy when I get home; it was recent. I bought one book. I got home by train. I had ended up near Trafalgar Square (intentionally), which was very crowded. I decided to get back to Herne Hill via Farrington, because I knew the way from there. It was satisfying to get back successfully, without considering whether there was a "better way".

Not all those who wander are lost.

The Fellowship of the Ring, J.R.R. Tolkien

Chapter 4: An experience of being lost

Next day (Friday). My daily goals seem modest. I walked to Brixton so I could go to the White Horse Inn on Brixton Road. As easy as this trip was, I am still struggling with Google Maps. But there is also my blindnesses. I walked straight past it without seeing it because I was expecting it to be on the corner of a street, based on photos I had looked at on Google ages ago. Perhaps I was wrong about that part. So, I walked about a kilometre past the pub before I turned back. But it was a sunny and very warm day, so it was okay.

Why would I want to see the White Horse Inn? It had to do with one of my great great grandfathers and a story my mother told me. William Archer was a convict. That makes three in my family: three of my sixteen great great grandparents were convicts. They were all tried and sentenced in or near London.

William was my first ancestor to come to Australia, on the *Waterloo* in 1838. He served out his sentence in the Hunter Valley, working for a farmer. He married Ellen Welch (a free settler, an assisted migrant), and they had eight children. Then, in the late 1860s, they packed up and went back to England, the only ancestors of mine to do so. They had an orchard in Kent. They spent about five years there, and then decided that Australia was a better option. They came back in 1874.

Subsequently, William had a hotel constructed at Pyrmont (in Sydney) and he became the publican. It was called the Duke of Edinburgh. So, you might ask, where does the white horse come in?

This is where my mother's story is relevant. She told me, when I was a child, that the hotel (she knew the name of it) had a white horse – whatever that meant. Was it a painting, was it a statue? I never knew, and people I have spoken to who knew the hotel told me there was never any white horse.

But, I looked at where William and family were staying, at Wilmington in Kent, on a map. I find it hard to believe that they never visited London during the time they lived there. And if they went from Wilmington to London, they would have gone past the White Horse Inn. Still, you might ask, so what?

Where William had grown up, at Harpenden in Hertfordshire, there was also a White Horse Inn. It is even possible that William worked there as a groom. So, the sight of the White Horse Inn at Brixton would have reminded him of his youth at Harpenden.

When I looked at a photo of the Duke of Edinburgh Hotel at Pyrmont in its early days (it was built in 1880), it looked very similar to the hotel at Brixton. Note, I checked that the hotel at Brixton existed at the time the Archer family lived at Wilmington. The windows were all arched and the stonework was decorated; I had seen photos of it from that time. It did raise the question for me, whether William was dreaming of building a hotel, and here was a worthy model. I wanted to see it for myself.

It is now a modern pub but quaint. It is still the same building from the mid-1800s. There is a narrow lane beside it that goes into a garage that fixes cars. One assumes that this was the passage through to the stables in the old days. The architecture of the building is in essence similar to the Duke of Edinburgh in Pyrmont, but the Brixton pub is more ornate. I went to a café across the road and had a wrap and coffee, and took some photos of it from there. It was very satisfying.

I walked down to Brixton station and caught the train to London Victoria station. I am managing the trains, but I still have to check which direction I am going.

I wanted to check where I was going to catch the bus to Oxford on Monday. I walked to a bus terminal, but the Oxford bus does not leave from there. I asked a man at the office, and he told me to walk along Buckingham Palace Road and it was Stop 10. I walked down there, remembering that I will have a suitcase and backpack, and it was indeed Stop 10. I asked a man about the journey and he was helpful.

I did more walking: through Pimlico, across the Thames, to the Battersea Power Station. I decided to catch buses to get back to Herne Hill. I was using Google Maps to determine the route. The buses were crowded. This was about 2:00 pm. The neighbourhood was all low-rise housing, relatively flat. I changed buses at Bedford Road, in accordance with Google. The second bus went towards Brixton. However, near Brixton I got off because it seemed the wrong direction and not near where I felt I needed to be. I walked towards what I thought was Herne Hill, but the directions didn't make sense.

It was that experience where it says twenty minutes, and you walk for ten minutes, then it says you are twenty minutes from your destination. A few times I walked a kilometre and then walked all the way back again. I think I was near Tulse Hill, which is south of Herne Hill. After an hour or more of this, I just stopped. I had walked backwards and forwards several times, and I had no idea at all of how to get found. I felt so stumped that I could take not another step, in any direction.

I feel lost in the city.

Jon Anderson, Heart of the Sunrise, Fragile (album)

An old lady walked past, with a buggy which she was pushing, with a three-year-old child in it, black. The lady was white. She asked me if I was okay. I asked her for directions to Herne Hill Station. She thought she could help me. She had a thick accent: Geordie? I knew it wasn't from around London.

She had to go into the flats to see her daughter; the child was her grandchild. She said for me to wait for her to come back. She was about five minutes. I waited. I still had no idea; nothing became clearer in those five minutes.

When the lady came back she said she would walk me to where I would know where I was. It was across a huge park. (It made me think of Centennial Park.) I had been walking in exactly the opposite direction to what I should have. She talked continually, and the child babbled happily and sang songs. We went into the park and walked right across it, and then we were near Herne Hill station. The park was an idyll: the trees created the shape of the landscape, the lawns were extensive, there was a large pond and a high hill. There were English birds I knew and some I did not know.

The lady stopped to have a cigarette, although she was short of breath. There was an ice cream truck and the lady wanted to buy one for the child (who was called Shandy) and I bought it for her. We walked down the hill and then I could see we were coming up to the rail station, and she left me. Her name was Elaine.

The whole episode was a surreal experience. Later, I found out that the park had been owned privately, by a family. There was a manor house in the middle of the land. Then, in the mid-twentieth century it became available for purchase, and people raised money so it could be purchased by the local council. I think there was a vibrancy about the park that felt like everyone was enjoying the space because it was somewhere from which they used to be excluded.

If you come to a fork in the road, take it.

Yogi Berra

On Saturday I went with my hosts to Wilmington, Kent: the place where William Archer and Ellen Welch and most of their children lived from about 1870 to late 1874. In the 1871 Census they appear, living along a lane near the Game Cock Inn. Wiliam had 3 ¼ acres of orchard. His ownership status is not known. But we did discover a heritage centre which was built in 2014. Unfortunately it was closed. It only opens twice a month, and today was not the day. We also found information about a history trail around the locality, and there is a web page with information about the various landmarks.

There was no Game Cock pub, but it would have been where there is post-war housing. It was next to a building called The Retreat. This was a school at the time when the Archers were living there, and it was near to where the lane would have been. So I realised for the first time that the children would have gone to school here.

The next day (it was Sunday), in the afternoon, I walked downtown, and on the way back I dropped into the church that was near to the place where I was staying. The door was open. A young lady invited me to come in. There was an area set up directly inside the door for an informal service and the eating of food. There were 3-4 people setting up equipment and being busy in the kitchen.

Beyond this was the church proper: pews, stained glass, spiritual space. The lady asked me if I belonged to a church, and where I was from, although the moment I open my mouth it is obvious I am Australian. She had been with this church for about five years. I said the church seemed alive, vibrant. She liked that.

I told her about family history, and the stories I had uncovered. My father's mother had been in an asylum for 35 years. She was admitted following the birth of her last child. She died in the institution. I have written about this. I said I wrote books, and I was wandering about England lost, just thinking about what I would write next.

Chapter 5: Getting lost in Oxford

I was leaving London for Oxford. I needed to travel by train into the city, then find the bus to Oxford. At the rail station I was confronted with three electronic signboards, but I am becoming more adept at deciphering the messages. I saw that most trains go to St Albans, and that the one to London Victoria (my destination) was cancelled, so I had to wait forty-five minutes. Fortunately, I will still have time to catch the bus, as I had planned for such events.

I have also learned to ask for help before I get to the point of desperation. At London Victoria station, I found an information person and asked her for directions to the bus stand. She directed me, and also gave me a bottle of water (free). That was a lifesaver for the trip.

When I got to the bus stand, a bus was already there, with a driver. I had my details ready: the email had been sent to my Gmail, which had the QR code. I was happy just to get this much right. After me, a group of three young people had trouble showing their tickets, for technological reasons, and it was obviously stressful.

Getting out of northern London was slow for the bus, as the traffic was heavy, but once the fields opened up, the going was quite fast. I watched for a long time, then read more of my book. The surroundings were mostly a hedgerow of trees. Occasionally a field of grass could be seen. There were no watercourses that I could see, or any big hills.

The bus was about half-full, and the driver stopped frequently to pick people up or let them off. After about two hours we arrived at Oxford. Where would I get off? The bus drove through the city, and stopped many times, so I wasn't sure. In the end, I just got off, and that wasn't a bad idea, as the shortest route to the Airbnb I had booked into is from mid-town. I had done my homework; I was prepared. I was still lugging my bags, but there was a café just across the road, and I went there, put the bags down, and had some lunch: a perfectly acceptable salad.

There was a lot to see in Oxford. I needed to walk around the town slowly and look at all the buildings, bearing in mind that among my ancestors is a family of stonemasons who lived just north of Oxford. The stonework is lush, and there is a massive amount of it. The stones on some of the buildings are very weathered; I wonder how old they are? However, the buildings I had seen in London with weathered stone tended to have a cruder design, whereas the stonework in Oxford is all impressive and ornate.

It probably took me an hour to walk to the flat where I am staying. I walked along an outer-suburbs-type road in a large semi-circle, past many flats, then some houses and gardens. I went past the Islamic Institute. Over the road from the flats is a Scout Hall with a large external sign: Be Prepared. I thought, with a touch of irony, I am trying. I am doing my best.

I put my gear down and started to walk back into town. Two routes were suggested by Google. The second route was along foot-tracks and through fields, so I took that, in honour of the Boy Scouts. I thought I was getting better at reading Google maps, but apparently I am not. I was walking between two high hedges, and I couldn't see into the distance. I had little idea about what the correct direction was. A ladybird landed on my hand as I stood still for a moment, and stayed there for a while, until I thought I'd better return it to the wild.

There were lots of nettles in the undergrowth. I remembered nettles from when I lived at Horseshoe Creek (Kyogle). There were clumps of them in various places. I used to pick them (wearing gloves) and put them in vegetable soups in wintertime. It gave a wholesome taste (and no, they do not sting after they have been cooked, and they are full of iron.)

A girl (meaning, early twenties) had walked in from a different track, and I stopped her (I am getting better at this) and asked her how to get to town. I admitted I was lost, but said what I had seen was delightful. However, I needed to get found at some point. She was sweet but she said, "You are going the wrong way." She pointed out the correct track, and gave me directions: go down that way, keep left, cross a small bridge over the stream, then turn right, etc.

I walked on happily. About ten minutes later I saw her again. She called out to me and came up to me. She said, "You are going the wrong way again. I saw you from over there, and I thought I had better rescue you. You're in my debt now."

I said that was okay. She walked with me for five minutes, and left me at an intersection with firm directions. I asked her if she lived in Oxford, and she said not anymore, but her parents were both academics: chemists, so she had grown up here. She said she had several brothers and sisters, and none of them had any interest in chemistry. I said I found that curious from a family history perspective.

I did eventually cross two footbridges, walk through a park and get to a part of the town. Then I thought about the bookshop Blackwells. I thought I should try to find that.

I am still having problems using Google Maps. I go the opposite way to what I should.

The wanderer's constancy brings good fortune.

I Ching, 35, Margaret Pearson

I found a bookshop and went in, and this time I did find a book I had to have. The book was called *Jude the Obscure*. I knew it was a novel by Thomas Hardy, whom I quite liked. Later, I looked it up on Wikipedia. It says: *Jude the Obscure* is a novel by Thomas Hardy, which began as a magazine serial in December 1894 and was first published in book form in 1895 (though the title page of my copy says 1896). The protagonist, Jude Fawley, is a working-class young man; he is a stonemason who dreams of becoming a scholar. The other main character is his cousin, Sue Bridehead, who is also his central love interest. The novel is concerned in particular with issues of class, education, religion, morality and marriage. It was Hardy's fourteenth and last published novel.

So, Jude the Obscure was a stonemason, and he loved his cousin! (Just like Charles Eaglestone, 1819-1911, a great great grandfather in my family, who married Elizabeth Eaglestone, the daughter of his father's brother.)

I returned to walking down the street, hopefully towards Blackwells, when I found another bookshop: "The Last Bookshop Jericho"; it's on Jericho Street. It was a mixture of old and new books; not a big shop, but it has a basement as well as the ground floor. I looked downstairs, looking for I Ching books, but there was nothing.

But, I found a book which was a history of stonemasons, for five pounds. I may very well learn something from that. It was a good find. I continued walking towards the city centre, and eventually I got there. There was a plaza, a place with no cars. I saw a tourist information centre, so I went in there and asked how I could get to Kirtlington and Bletchington, the two villages where the Eaglestone families lived. She looked it up using Google, and then wrote instructions for me on the back of a map of Oxford. There is a bus that goes to both places!

The next day I was thinking about the two villages, but I needed to see Oxford first. I walked into town, along the tracks for pedestrians and cyclists, crossing the river (the Thames, I think). I did not get lost this time, although I still have only a rudimentary sense of map-and-compass.

It is quite something to be surrounded by this wealth of stonework and ornamentation, being in courtyards with the walls of buildings on all sides. I keep thinking about what part the Eaglestone men may have played in all this.

I went in search of Blackwells, the bookshop. There is a Waterstones as well. I went into a Blackwells store, but it was entirely manga and sci-fi. I asked the man at the counter, and he explained that there were several Blackwells shops: this one, one for children's books, and one that was more comprehensive. The latter was just over the road, so I went there. One section was just for music.

Inside, there were various levels, like a series of mezzanine floors, stepping down below the street. I didn't try to size up everything; one gets exhausted too easily in that attempt. I went to the Philosophy and Religion sections. I looked for I Ching books, and there were six of them. And all of them were in my library at home.

I bought one book: *When we cease to understand the world*. I noted that Rutger Bregman's new book, *Moral Ambition*, is being promoted. He wrote the book, *Humankiind: A Hopeful History* (2019). I have both books. The former I found at a recent book fair in Sydney. There was also a book about why Christianity has been pushed aside; however, although his argument was somewhat attractive, he wrote from within a Christian worldview, that is, without any sense of the legitimate place of other religions.

I am accumulating books. I will have to ship some home.

I went to the Waterstones store to see if they had any I Ching books. They did not. The shopgirl showed me their one book on Chinese philosophy, the *Tao Te Ching*, although she didn't know what it was. So, the evidence is accumulating that the I Ching is fading from knowledge.

I walked past a hat shop: it just sold hats. It was full of hats of many kinds: traditional types (I know they all have names, but all I know is "bowler"!). Still in business in Oxford. And the building was a Tudor building that looked hundreds of years old.

Next to it was the Church of St Michael. The tower (currently being restored) was from 1100 AD. Inside was beautiful. Stained glass windows, not huge. A small statue of a dragon being slain by a knight with a sword.

After food, I thought I needed to see more of Oxford. I wondered about the old city wall, and I hadn't seen inside a college. I walked, with only a minimal sense of direction, and came upon a building that looked interesting. It was the Sheldonian Theatre, a round, domed building in the middle of a square. I paid for admission. This is the place where students come at the beginning of their course, and at the end, for graduation. I like the idea of a gathering to honour the commencement of a course. I have never experienced that at an Australian university.

When travelling, don't plan the route.

Chinese proverb

The word "theatre" misled me. It has nothing to do with the theatre, only with pageantry, I suppose. The building was designed by Christopher Wren, who designed St Paul's Cathedral, and about fifty other churches and public buildings after the great fire in 1666. This building comes from the same era. Christopher Wren was a busy man.

This building had a stairway to the top of the dome, from where you can see all of Oxford. It is 128 steps to the top level, nothing compared to the 500+ steps that I walked up at St Paul's in London. It is a circular staircase. You end up in a room which has all the heavy timbers of a roof. Then there is a smaller climb to the top, which is not open. There are eight glass windows, with the directions named (North, South, East, West). It gives you a magnificent view over the city. What struck me was that it was above all the surrounding spires, and there were so many, it was like standing in a forest of spires.

After this exploration I walked on, to the North, and I saw one of those enclosed bridges that go between two buildings. I have a picture at home of one at Cambridge, which was in a calendar my mother brought back years ago from her trip to England. I took pictures of this one, then walked down the lane. After some turns, I came to New College, and it was open. I paid for admission.

There was a quadrangle to start with, mown grass in the centre, and one tree at the side, and some jasmine vines in one part. Then I went into the Chapel. It was extraordinary. The stone columns must have been 100 feet high. There was an anteroom, which was large enough to house a concert, and there were chairs stacked up on the side for that purpose. There was the main interior, which was a church designed for choirs and singing. The altar section had a series of statues of people: five levels of thirteen statues, with elaborate stonework in between the levels. Down each side were tall stained-glass windows with more images of people. I don't know the meaning.

The pews faced the middle, and they were tiered. It was an amazing space.

Next, I saw a refectory room, with the places all laid out ready for a meal. There must have been seats for 200 people. The kitchen was next to it, an industrial cooking space. I can't imagine sitting down to eat every night with 200 other people. The logistics alone would be daunting, and the caged aspect would haunt me.

I walked towards the far end of the campus. There was an open gate and lawns beyond. One of the college people spoke to me, a man in his fifties perhaps. He suggested I go out to the garden, when I would also see the old city wall, dating from before medieval times. I remembered that I had wanted to see this. He said he had a sister-in-law living in Sydney, but doesn't that mean that his brother is living there too? Life is full of more things that I don't understand.

I saw the old wall, perhaps 30-40 feet high, rougher stonework than in the buildings. Along the wall there was an old garden, but it was well-kept. Many flowers I did not recognise. It was beautiful. High up in the wall there were many vantage points from where archers would have shot arrows at the enemy. The openings were tall and thin, perhaps no more than an inch wide, but 18 inches high, and chamfered on the inside to allow the archers to point in different directions. I wondered about where William Archer's family obtained their surname.

There was a residential building on the far side, a modern building. I walked the circle to come back to the quadrangle, and walked back down the lane. I got lost again. But I stopped and had afternoon tea. I gradually found myself again.

Chapter 6: A quick trip to Bletchington

I departed from Oxford. With my full load, I walked the forty minutes along the walking track into town and to the rail station. I asked about storage lockers, because otherwise I could not take the trip on the bus to Bletchington, but they had no lockers. However, the man said there was storage at the nearby youth hostel which, fortunately, I had just passed, so I knew where it was.

So, I bought a ticket to Bath for this afternoon. I had decided that I could not make it to both Bletchington and Kirtlington, so I decided on the former only. I went back to the youth hostel to store my two bags. Ironically it was up a narrow flight of stairs, but I managed. It cost me ten pounds, but it was essential.

The weather has stayed warm and reasonably clear, not too hot.

The bus trip was easy enough. Flat country, fields and some trees. Big bus, narrow road. We went through Gosford (on the outskirts of Oxford), and Hampton Poyle (rural). At Bletchington, we stopped right outside the Black's Head Inn, where I alighted. The inn was closed. It is on the main road, an old stone building. I think it still operates as a pub. [Benjamin Bullock (1787-1856), was the publican of the Black's Head Inn. He was also the Census-taker, he occasionally conducted wedding ceremonies, and he taught at the local school, a man of many hats. He is of relevance because he married Mary Eaglestone, the sister of Thomas and Edward, but she died young. Thomas was the father of Charles, my great great grandfather.]

I wanted to see St Gile's church. It is not in the town,; it is about a mile to the north. (I feel that perhaps I am acquiring some sense of north and south.) I started to walk down one road, unsure of my directions. I came across a man walking a dog, so I asked him. He knew. He had an accent; I can't name it, but not local to here. He was amusing. He said to walk back to the intersection, cross the road – carefully – and walk behind the stone bus shelter and veer left. It's down that road. Far more precise than he needed to be.

Advantageous to step into the great stream.

I Ching, 13, Richard Wilhelm

Everything around me is stonework: all the houses, and long stretches of stone walls. Some walls are four feet high, some are eight feet high, with a jagged course of stones pointing up all along the tops. Even in a new estate I saw, the design has copied the old; only the stones are shiny new and yellowish. There were a few people around, just occasionally. I walked past a building called the Old Rectory, and I had a look at that. I think it is some kind of centre now, maybe for children. After this, the road became more rural, but there was a sign indicating that a church was ahead.

The church was over a mile from town. I walked along the road with views to the distance of undulating hills and fields. No intense cropping that I could see. Coming up to the church there were some houses, most of which were old, and most were big, and of stone. A few were new. There seem to be some big estates, then smaller holdings clustered between them.

There was a narrow roadway up the incline to the church. There are so many trees around it that you cannot see it at all until you are quite close. There is a carpark, gravel, and low fences around the church yard and the two cemeteries: an old one around the church, and the other closer to the carpark. I looked through the first cemetery. It was smallish, with modern burials only. Men were mowing the grass and brush cutting, so it was noisy. There was a freshly dug grave, with a temporary wooden cover over it and a huge pile of soil beside it.

Then I entered the church yard where the church was situated. It was now visible, and there was a gravel drive up to it for pedestrians. The square tower of the church was formidable, and very old; was it Norman? There was a vestibule on the side, then a big dark door. I thought it was closed, but I could push it open. I looked inside the church. It was dark and the roof was very high: high walls, high roof, tall stained-glass windows.

I knew that many ceremonies of the Eaglestones have been held in this church: baptisms, marriages and funerals.

It was just outside this door that I found something wonderful. Besides the path leading up to the entrance, I was looking at the names on all the gravestones, and I immediately recognised the name Elizabeth Eaglestone! It was Charles Eaglestone's first wife. Elizabeth was his cousin, the daughter of his father's brother. She died on 11 March 1851 of scarlet fever. I looked at the gravestones around it, but there were no familiar names, so I don't think there was a family section.

When I looked around the back of the churchyard, it was all overgrown, and few of the gravestones were legible. So, I am taking the sighting of Elizabeth Eaglestone's grave as a gift. Her death was significant because it was the trigger for Charles to join up with Hannah Palmer, and for their decision to come to Australia.

When Elizabeth got sick, Hannah came over to nurse her. Hannah's father had been a stonemason too, so everyone was known to each other and they seemed to be neighbourly. But Elizabeth did not recover. This was the way of it with scarlet fever in those days. I wonder if it was Charles who carved her gravestone. It was a couple of years later when Charles and Hannah married. Edwin, their son (my great grandfather), was two years old when they emigrated to Australia.

On the way back to town I was passed by two ladies going for a ride on horseback.

It was not possible today to go to Deamond Farm, where some of the Eaglestones lived, or to go to Kirtlington. For that, one would need a car or a lot more time. So, I waited for the bus to return to Oxford.

Adorning the feet, leaving the car and walking. This is to embrace the Tao, content with no external artifice. One knows one's knowledge is limited, therefore one seeks.

I Ching, 22, Thomas Cleary

Back at Oxford, I had lunch at a Korean restaurant. That tasted good. The young waiter asked me where I was from. I said Australia. He asked me where in particular. I said Sydney. Again, he asked me where. I said Hornsby. He said, "Ooh, that's nice." I asked him how he knew. He said he was born in Sydney and grew up there. I asked him if he liked living in England. He said, "No, not enough sunlight."

At the rail station there were crowds, including groups of schoolchildren. And they have different carriages on the train, so you have to be conscious of that too: first class, standard, cycles etc. I managed to get on alright. I had two changes on the way to Bath: Didcot Parkway and Bristol Parkway. At Didcot Parkway I had to carry my bag up the stairs to the next platform. I managed. I was glad I had limited myself to a smallish suitcase.

I got off at Oldfield Park, the stop before Bath. I saw on Google Maps that it was closer to the Airbnb I had booked than Bath Spa station. The walk to the Airbnb was about ten minutes. As I got out of the train it started to shower, but not too heavily, and it stopped after a few minutes. There was a ramp up to the overhead bridge that I had to cross; no steps. I only made one wrong turn on my way. I am sure this is admissible. I had to stop and check again, somewhat slowly and painstakingly, but successfully.

Again, I am about 20-30 minutes from town. I am getting lots of walking. I feel a bit fitter. I went down the road for dinner. There were choices. I chose a Thai place: Thailand Wok. After the meal, I realised I did not have my wallet. I hadn't worn my jacket, and I had forgotten to take my wallet out of the jacket pocket. I explained this, and they were okay about it. I walked back (five minutes) and retrieved it, and went back and paid my debt. I can walk with my head held high again.

I walked downtown, remembering that it stays light until around ten o'clock, because I wanted to know where I needed to go tomorrow. I have booked a tour to Stonehenge. The place was the Abbey Hotel. It is right at the top of town, which has impressive buildings, including the hotel itself, and a building called The Architect. There are squares and plazas: places with no cars, which have a nice feel.

I was told that the University of Bath has a great reputation, so that many students come here. I think I am an outsider, not part of that world. My path did not take me into work at universities until later in life, so that that could be called just a pre-retirement job. At a certain point I decided I was outside of the accepted hierarchy of knowledge.

At Oxford yesterday, at New College, I heard two men talking. One was saying he was a bit rushed because he had been asked to give a talk this afternoon on some topic to some group. That was the way of things. I am not so assigned.

I say to people: I am a non-joiner, but they are not quite the right words. I could say, "I have left institutions behind." But then, that sounds pretentious. And I don't even need to say that. I don't need to say anything at all.

On the way back from town (still light at 8 pm, a long slow fading light) I followed Google. It took me up a narrow alley, through a tunnel underneath the train lines, and up a narrow pathway to the next road. But I had to keep the app open, following it step by step, rather than thinking what the major turns were and putting it away.

At Blackwells bookshop I had bought a book, *When we cease to understand the world*, and I am reading that. It is challenging, but then I read the I Ching and it seems to offer a personal resolution.

Chapter 7: Seeing Stonehenge and Bath

This afternoon I have a tour booked to Stonehenge. This morning it is raining. Weather occurs. I spent two hours trying to work out plans for going to Waterford. I have booked a plane from Bristol to Dublin. I wanted to follow the path that Sarah Crosby went in about 1846, in reverse, but it was too complicated for the time I have available. She went from Waterford to Bath, as many Irish people did at that time, even before the potato famine struck. They went there to work, and there was a slum part of the city where they congregated: Avon Street.

I would have liked to have taken the ferry. You can still go from Fishguard, on the west coast of Wales, to Rosslare Harbour in Wexford. But one needs to get to Fishguard, so it involves several connections to get you from Bath to Waterford. Instead, I am taking the easier way, by plane from Bristol to Dublin.

The rest still has to be worked out.

I walked downtown in the rain. I am still unsure of the way. I stopped in a doorway to consult my phone again when a young man poked his head out, wondering if I was wanting to enter the shop. It was some kind of physical therapy clinic. As I have done on numerous occasions, I asked for his advice. He was kindly. I had already gone a different way to yesterday, and his directions got me close to my destination, the Abbey Hotel.

I had two hours until the tour. I wandered around close to the hotel, but this seems to be the central tourist/historical area. I saw the outside of the Roman Baths, and the Abbey, a huge church with a squarish disposition. I may go there tomorrow.

I wondered where Avon Street was. It was close by. Then I saw a huge tree, a maple which must have been 200 years old, or more. It is in the middle of a square. I tried to get a decent photograph of it. It is difficult to hold an umbrella, fend off the rain, and position the phone to take a picture.

I walked a bit more and saw another tree in another square. There was a group of visitors being lectured to by a man, a tourist guide I assume, under the tree. An old lady walked past me. She saw that I was looking at the tree, and she spoke to me. She said the tree was around 500 years old. It is a plane tree, and it was brought to Bath from China, the first plane tree in England.

[Later, at home: I looked it up on the internet. There is a web page devoted to the tree. It is a plane tree, but it is not 500 years old. Most of this can be worked out from the many maps available of the Abbey Green Quarter going back as far as 1100 AD, where the green is shown open, without a main tree in the centre.

[There are many stories about the tree, which is right in the middle of a movie set for the "Bridgerton" (American-made) series. It is also the subject of "many a dark spooky tale", including the most famous and widely repeated tale of it being used for hangings, thus it is known as the Hanging Tree. There are stories that witches were tortured and hung there too.

[However, a watercolour painting by James Blackamore dated 1785 reveals a large Green surrounded by cobbles but no tree. Some sources say it was planted as a sapling in 1793, while others say the tree was not actually planted until the 1880s, as maps show it was not there in 1852, but first features on an 1888 map. So, it could be from 140 to 230 years old, still profoundly impressive.

[There are also photographs of the tree over the years. One photo, taken in 1911, shows it as a "smallish tree".]

I wanted to know something about the lady who had taken the time to tell me this wonderful story about the tree (even if it turned out to be not exactly true). She told me that she was eighty-three, and she had come to Bath when she was sixty. She went to Bath University to study astronomy, astrology and their effect on culture. I told her I had studied for a Diploma of Family History during covid. And I told her about my great great grandmother, an Irish girl, who had come to Bath during the potato famine.

[Yes, when I was back at home, I wondered about courses in astronomy, astrology and culture. I found the Sophia Centre for the Study of Cosmology in Culture. It is at the University of Wales Trinity Saint David. It offers an MA in Cultural Astronomy and Astrology, and it has a Faculty of Astrological Studies, established 1948. It says it is unique in that it is the only university degree in the world to feature the history, culture and theory of astrology. So, it would seem possible that what the lady told me is true in some sense, and that the University of Bath provided her with an opportunity to pursue that interest.]

There was a bookshop near to the Abbey Hotel, in an old building with stone columns, and a staircase at the front. It was lovely. Its history was as the meeting place for the Society of Friends, the Quakers. The present occupant was Topping & Company, Booksellers. There was a ground floor and a basement. It was all laid out in small alcoves. I found the Philosophy/Religion section, and there were three I Ching books: Wilhelm, Minford and Brian Browne Walker. For a small selection, I approved; I would have added Huang.

The tour group to Stonehenge consisted of twelve people on a small bus. It was raining lightly when we boarded. The tour was from 2:00 pm to 6:00 pm, and the driver (Dan) kept to time. It was an hour's drive. I think this area is close to perfect England (my perception): green, undulating hills with groves of trees. There are small villages whose names I had never heard of between Bath and Stonehenge (henge = hedge (roughly)).

At Stonehenge there was a large carpark and a separate place for buses. There were about twenty buses parked there. But this, apparently, is not the busy time. Dan sorted out our tickets, then we left him and we caught another bus which took us the last mile to the stones. This bus was crowded. When we got there, the rain and wind suddenly intensified. I had brought my umbrella (purchased in London) and that was good. However, the wind and rain were fierce, and the legs of my jeans still got very wet.

It only lasted about 5-10 minutes. I don't read a message into it, but it has to be said that when I got to Stonehenge, it rained fiercely.

The rope forbidding access is around ten metres from the stones. All around the stones, for a kilometre or more, is grass. Most of it is left unmown, but it still looks tame, only about one foot high, sprinkled with the heads of purple flowers.

I took photos all around the stones, at intervals of about thirty degrees. All the views are different. Later, in the visitor centre, I saw that all of the stones had had capstones and they linked together to form a complete circle. And the standing stones (sarsens) had small mounds at the top so that they pinned the capstones in place.

There are four or five capstones still in place now. Some others are on the ground. There is one stone which is separate from the circle. It stands in the ground, but it is on an angle, and it is not a finished shape. This arrangement of stones is part of a much bigger scheme, which has circles and avenues that extend all the way to the sea (according to the book on Stonehenge at my hosts' place that I had looked at). Yet, the original meaning of it all is unknown.

There are theories and propositions: It had meaning; it was religious; the druids came and used them; maybe there were ceremonies here, and festivals, and maybe sacrifices. The alignment of the stones with the compass directions has been noted.

Today it still seems significant, and it goes against our idea of the evolution of humanity, from primitive hunters and gathers to agricultural people, then onto villages, cities and industrial development: civilisation.

The assumed trajectory is that we have progressed from primitive to sophisticated, that our understanding has continually increased. But then you get a book like that which I am reading now: when we no longer understand the world (by Labatut). It argues that our knowledge of the world is stumbling into uncertainty, disintegrating. However, he is not really addressing the long-term trajectory of knowledge.

One of the books I have written, *Future*, suggests that we should doubt the trajectory of continuous growth. Obviously our scientific and technological knowledge has grown in the last few hundred years, but there is vast evidence of spectacular achievements much further into the past that we have no explanation for. We should not deride this past or think that we understand it completely.

The other day, in Herne Hill, I was walking along the footpath when I saw the pieces of a jigsaw scattered on the ground. That is a great metaphor. I think it comes close to encapsulating the state of our knowledge.

From the stones, I walked along a track back to the visitor centre instead of catching the bus. Half of the walk was across the field, and half of it was through forest. The forest was soft underfoot and gentle after the rain. Unlike the grassy field, there were many birds in the forest.

On the drive back to Bath, the driver pointed out where a white horse can be seen on a hillside, formed into the slope. I saw the spot, but it was too misty to make it out properly. It reminds me of the story mum told me about a white horse being associated with the Duke of Edinburgh hotel (that William Archer built and ran).

After we returned to Oxford I walked home, late afternoon, no rain, still some water on the ground here and there. I did not get lost.

Tomorrow, I have an entire day to see Bath, and I do not have to move house. On Saturday morning I will go early so I can get to Bristol.

The traveller does not tarry long in one place.

I Ching, 35, Margaret Pearson

Today I need to package up and send off some of the books, to get rid of the bulk and weight of them from my luggage. I found my way to the post office. The price to send the package to Australia was just under 40 pounds. Ah well. I had to fill in the customs form, and put my Bath address. The girl said I had to put the postcode too, but when I asked her what it was, she didn't know. Maybe they have many postcodes in the one town. Or is everyone just as lost as I am?

I made my way to the Abbey to go on a tour. I had time to look through the ground floor of the church, which is grand. It is very tall, and the stained-glass windows go all the way up. The side walls are lined with plaques commemorating notable people who had died. Most of the names seemed to belong to the 1700s and 1800s. I think there was even one for Beau Brommel, the dandy.

When I first learned that some people in my family tree were stonemasons, I simply thought of gravestones. But now I see the extraordinary scope of the work they did. They built this whole city. It involved great engineering knowledge, and a wide range of practical skills. It involved intricate designs and fine art, working at great heights, and also demanded sophisticated construction skills, for example, the ability to manoeuvre large weights into place at heights.

The guided tour up to the bell tower was conducted by two guides. There were steep steps winding about a central axis, just as in St Paul's in London and the Sheldonian Theatre at Oxford. I think this time there were 218 steps. First, we came to the room where the bellringers do their work. There are ten bells. They ring a peel; they don't call it a tune.

The bells hang on a central axis and rock backwards and forwards when the ropes are pulled. The heaviest bell is 1.7 tonnes. There is also a small rack of ropes that allows small hammers to strike the bells. This makes a softer sound, but one person can do it, and you can do fast runs.

There was a long peel for the marriage of King Charles III and Camilla that went for three hours. This doesn't happen very often. Normally the bells are rung twice a week. The youngest bell-ringer is fifteen and the oldest is eighty-two. They have to climb the stairs.

The ropes come through a central point in the ceiling and fan out in a circle. The ends form loops. The bell-ringers use a long steel rod with a hook on the end which hooks onto the looped ropes. I asked how this was different from a carillon, but it's just a different setup (carillons have a quasi-keyboard) which allows the person to play tunes.

We walked through a small door and along a walkway to see where the clock is. There is a clock mechanism in the bell-ringers' room. It is now electric. Up until 1979 the clock was mechanical, and was wound up twice a week. We also went into the dark, cramped space where the bells are hung, and saw the bells.

We walked higher up, and now we were outside, and we walked along for a while, then back inside and higher up again. We got to a flat space with a parapet all round and ornate towers in each corner. There was a flagpole in the middle. From here you can see 360-degrees: all of Bath. Nearby was another church with a spire that is twenty metres taller. It was the Roman Catholic church, built in the 1860s. So, it was not here when Sarah Crosby was here.

I asked the guide about this, and he said that in 1848 there was no Roman Catholic church in Bath. There were still laws restricting the Catholic faith. The church existed in an informal way in the city.

The guide told us the history of the church, and the machinations of King Henry VIII, selling off things from the church, including its bells, to pay for the wars he was involved in. The guide also spoke of bombing in World War 2. The church survived, but there was some damage to it, which has been restored.

There were more things to see. I saw the Roman Baths, but didn't feel obliged to go in. A couple, Muslims, asked me to take a photo of them with the Abbey in the background. I asked them to do the same for me. That's the first photo on this trip that contains me.

I wanted to see the Jane Austen Museum. That is, I walked around Bath lost for a while. It was the same issue: which way is north? Do I go left or right?

When he walked through the streets, he desired to have someone lead him by the hand.

Martin Martin (1655-1719) (no relation to me) visiting Glasgow from his home at St Kilda, on the remote island of Hirta, which is west of the Hebrides on the west coast of Scotland. [from Eric Newby, *A Book of Travellers' Tales*]

I suppose I have to say, eventually I found the Jane Austen Museum, but it left a niggle of annoyance. It was in the opposite direction from what I thought. The museum is in a house that is near to where she used to live in Bath, and similar in style. The actual house where she lived is owned by a dentist, who refused to sell it for the museum. A lady gave a talk about Jane Austen's life and family. It was one of Jane's brothers who revealed her authorship of her several novels, after her death.

[I have since discovered that there are Jane Austen museums in other towns, in places where she had also lived.]

She was born in 1775, and died at forty-one. The exhibit featured movies that have been made of her novels. There was a room set up as her writing room: it had a small desk with a quill pen. Her ideas came from people in the circle of her family, and people she saw in the social circles of Bath.

Most of the people attending the tour were female. There was the opportunity to dress up in costume. No, I did not do that.

Jane Austen wrote novels. I was fifteen when I read *Pride and Prejudice*, and it left an indelible mark on me: the elegance of her writing. "It is a truth universally acknowledged, that a single man in possession of a good fortune, must be in want of a wife." I even loved her commas.

There is grace and dignity in this opening passage of the book, but also a trace of self-mocking humour that prevents it from being pompous.

As a child, she wrote stories and read them out to her family. Her father, a vicar, encouraged her. She sought publication, but anonymously, just as "a woman". It was after her death that she began to be recognised. Why did she write?

I walked up the road and saw a bookshop: Persephone. It is both a bookshop and a publishing company. All the books looked similar. I asked the lady, and she said they print books by women, usually books that have been forgotten. They had some books by Monica Dickens, great great grand-daughter of Charles Dickens. Having just relieved myself of some books, I didn't purchase any books here.

The other thing I wanted to see was the Royal Crescent. I got lost again, but I did find it. It is such a grand semi-circle of joined houses. The architect was Sir John Wood, 1775. Imagine living in a home identical with twenty-nine others! But, the people lived in a great social circle, not just an architectural semi-circle, and there were frequent grand and gay events.

Could this have been where Sarah worked as a servant/maid, walking across town from Avon Street? (Later, she left Bath and went to London. Why? My theory is that she was looking for her brother, James, who may have been attempting to get to the Unites States, as many Irish did at this time. My evidence is scant; it shows up in the notes taken in Sarah's trial: that she had a brother called James. Filling in the gaps, I surmise that it was an older brother, and that he had got out of Ireland as well, after the potato famine started to devastate the crops in 1846.)

Chapter 8: To Waterford, with help

I packed my bags and vacated my room at the Airbnb. I wanted to leave the host a message, because she had been responsive and helpful, and the room was well-appointed, but the interface on Airbnb required me to validate myself in an absurd way. I gave my UK phone number and some other details, then it presented me with two pictures and asked me to move arrows to match the first screen with the second.

However, I couldn't make sense of the pictures. It was like a children's gaming screen, and I could never master the childish interface of computer games; nor did I have the patience or the interest to do so. I managed to complete the first "puzzle", but then it presented me with a second one, and apparently there were five of these, all required so that I could send a simple message.

I gave up. The baby technos have taken over. I was born before sliced bread, and it would do the baby technos good to remember this. There are some things that are beneath my dignity.

It was a thirty-minute walk to Dorchester Street near the rail station, hauling my suitcase. I managed to do it by a different route, not intentionally, but successfully. At no time was I lost.

This time I went through an underpass under the railway, and across a pedestrian bridge over the River Avon. Apparently, there are several rivers called Avon in England. And the word Avon itself means River.

I was at a big bus station, with sixteen departure places, but I could not find the correct stop. Eventually a man in a uniform came past, and I asked him, whether it was his job or not. The bus to Bristol Airport was not here, he said. It was down the road on the other side of the street. This person was the first of about ten people who helped me to get to my destination today, an Airbnb in Waterford. Each one of them was essential, and each one turned up at just the right time.

The bus, a double decker, was already waiting. The driver was a middle-aged woman. I had my ticket ready on my phone, with the QR code, and that was seamless. So, being prepared pays.

The bus went straight to Bristol Airport, so no changes were necessary. It stopped many times along the way. Some people were on short trips, others went a long way. The terrain was hilly, and it felt close, but there were fields of grass, and a few crops underway. Some sheep and cows too. The weather was overcast, with a few drops of rain, but it was more like atmosphere or mood than an event.

Bristol airport: it is on a high rise, so you don't really see it until you arrive. The place where the bus dropped us off was over a hundred metres from the entrance to the terminal, and now it did start to rain. I noted that there were other buses that stopped right outside the terminal.

There were hundreds of people; Saturday morning, I guess. Most of them were flying with Easy Jet. It gave the impression that it caters to people who have never travelled before, like it's a get-away chance for working people who don't have much money. The crowd looked like a cross-section of society, including young people who were all smarted up as if they were about to get their photo taken for Facebook, and the elderly who were joining the throng.

However, the passengers for Aer Lingus (which may also be called Ryan Air? I wasn't sure. Later: No) were a small bunch. I was early; I had to wait an hour, so I was reading a new book, having finished *When we cease to understand the world*. It's called *Wild Once*; it's about the way of witches, understood to mean, acknowledging nature in life. I don't like the word "witches", but the place of nature in life is fundamental. I also have to wait and see what she says about powers, spells and manipulation.

A bus drove us out to where the plane was. The plane was about two-thirds full, a small plane with propellers. It's a flight of about an hour to Dublin. I wanted to see the sea, but there was nothing to see. It was all cloud, all the way until we got to the coastline off Dublin. I think it was here that my timing as planned went astray. The plane was a bit late. My bus ticket was for a specific time, but I figured that it was valid for today, at whatever time I happened to arrive.

So, I wasn't worried about that. But did I miss the bus I had been planning on catching?

The bus area was very large and spread out, and I couldn't see where to go. There were so many buses! Some were going to further places, like Limerick, but there were also many buses going to Dublin City:

44

with different names, different colours, different companies. I asked one official for the Dublin Coaches area, and he said Station 16. I was getting closer. When I got to Station 16, it was an area for around ten buses. I was still unsure.

Also, critically, the internet on my phone was not working, so I couldn't check or confirm anything. I wasn't expecting this. However, I checked for available networks, and there was a free, accessible network for the airport. When I paused, there was an Irish girl waiting for a bus to one of the counties. She had a while to wait, she said, so she would accompany me and help me while she was there. I noticed there was a bus (JJ Kavanagh's) that went straight to Waterford. I did not know this was possible; I thought I had to go to Dublin first. Anyway, I already had a ticket and I would persevere with that.

I waited a long time. I asked the driver of one bus, and he said that the 750 would be along in fifteen minutes. The fifteen minutes stretched to over half an hour. The Irish girl went and talked to some people who were waiting, and she said some of them were waiting for a bus to Dublin city. I was having doubts. However, a double decker bus turned up and lots of people got on it. So did I.

The number of people who had helped me so far was about four.

When I got to the bus-stop for Dublin city, it wasn't in Dublin city. It was a bus area in the middle of nowhere. There was a new light rail station nearby. I suppose it went into the city. I spoke to a bus driver in a double decker bus, and I said I was going to Waterford. He said, "Get on". But then we drove two hundred metres down the road and through two roundabouts and he stopped.

"Ah," he said. "Did you mean Waterford City?" And he said, "You'd better get off and go back, and you'll get a bus from there." Two vehicles behind the bus were blasting us with their horns, because the driver had stopped the traffic. I walked back with my luggage to the bus area, which is called Red Cow Louas.

There were few other people around now. But there was a black guy in uniform, who explained he was waiting for two people. He had a private bus, maybe from a hotel. He said he would help me while he was waiting. He had an app that could track the buses live. But he said he couldn't see a bus on the way that was going to Waterford. Then his passengers arrived and he left.

Another bus turned up, a double decker that was going into Dublin city. Another woman driver. She didn't know about the Dublin Coaches bus, but she said her bus had free wifi, and she had ten minutes to wait until her next trip. I could sit on the bus and use the wifi. By this time, I was wondering whether I needed to start making disaster plans, that is, planning to stay the night in Dublin.

That was another set of options, and I would have to make the decision quickly, before the bus with the free wifi disappeared. I was still sitting with the situation when, lo and behold, another double decker bus arrived that was a 600, the right bus according to the notes I had written by hand in my notebook. And yes, it was the right bus. He was going to Waterford, and my ticket was accepted by the ticket reader. He had space down below for luggage.

The lady bus driver gave me a big wave.

We set off. The bus was smooth and fast. We headed south; I'm saying this based on the relative positions of Dublin and Waterford on a map. The sky was still overcast, and some of the time it was raining. I could just make out the light of the western sun. The terrain was similar to that of the England where I had been the last few days, but subtly different. Perhaps it looked less industrialised. I noticed more hills and rocks too.

It was now just after five pm, and the trip is about two hours, so I am hoping all goes smoothly when we get to Waterford. The bus stops; people get on and off, going short trips and long trips. We stop at Kilkenny, a town with old city walls with turrets, still standing proudly. Local people get off and on the bus.

We arrive at Waterford bus station right on seven pm. I am close to my destination. But then I discover I have no internet again, and there is no free service available. This means I can't message the Airbnb. Once again, I am lost. I do remember that the address is in Canada Street in the Newtown district. There is a waiting place for the buses, so I go in there, and find an employee to ask for help once again. He is a short man (meaning, shorter than me). He is very helpful, but he does not know Canada Street. He does know Newtown. He says there is no bus going in that direction, but am I okay walking? I am okay walking; I have been doing a lot of it.

I head off: the man's instruction was to go to the Tower Hotel, then veer left and you'll find someone and you can ask them for directions to Canada Street. It's about fifteen minutes. I haven't eaten at all today. I was going to eat at Bristol airport, but it was so crowded and hectic, I decided I didn't want to, and it was probably better if I didn't eat under those conditions.

I got to The Three Shippes Inn on the right. There was a side street. I looked, and couldn't see any name on the street. Three young girls were walking by. I asked them if they knew Canada Street. They said they didn't.

I walked on, about another kilometre, past a lovely park, very green grass and a low stone fence all around it, and up a hill towards a grand-looking college. Then a young man came along and I asked him the question about Canada Street. He knew, but he also checked on his phone and he showed me. Canada Street was back at the park. It was the street where I had spoken to the three girls. I wondered: did the girls honestly not know the name of the street where they were living? They were all Indian. Maybe they were here for study, and just needed to know how to physically get from the apartment to their college.

I walked down Canada Street, past the inn. It was all commercial buildings and private apartments on the right, with the park on the left. The street stopped and the park was still in front. I wondered if

47

the street continued after the park, which can happen in Sydney, so I walked through the park. The street did not continue, so I walked back to the intersection where the inn was. I walked up the other side of Canada Street. I could see very few numbers on the buildings, and those that were there didn't help.

For example, on the right, at the end, next to the river, was a hotel, and next to it were two houses labelled 1 and 2. At the door of the hotel, a young man walked out, so I asked him what this building was. He said it was a hotel, and a very nice one.

At this point I was thinking that maybe I would have to stay in the hotel, even though it was in the same street as the place I had booked. I had no way of contacting the owner. I walked back down the street, and stopped just outside a place. At least these places looked residential. So, my suitcase is parked on the ground, and I still have my backpack on. There is a Thai lady standing there, outside a Thai restaurant. She asks if I need help.

I tell her my quandary. She doesn't know the numbers in the street. I tell her I can't access the internet on my phone. She offers to connect her phone to mine as a hotspot so I can access the internet. Then a man turns up. He seems middle-eastern (if that appellation is still permissible). He lives nearby. He offers to help. We need a password for the internet, and he knows a bit more than her, so he takes her phone and looks.

Then, the three ladies that the Thai lady is waiting for show up. One of them is her daughter. She helps too, with the password business. And finally, I can send a message to the Airbnb guy. He says he will send someone down with the key. The ladies go into the Thai restaurant for dinner. The middle-eastern guy waits with me.

Two minutes later a young Irish guy shows up and he has the key to the apartment. It is now about 8:30 pm. He is cheerful, and he lets me in. He even carries my heavy suitcase up the three flights of stairs. And he fixes my phone. All he had to do was shift it to 'data roaming'. I don't understand why this has surfaced as a problem, but I am a bit tired after my long day.

The apartment is on the top floor and is at the corner of the street. It has a large window that overlooks the park diagonally opposite. I set down my luggage, wash my face and hands and head straight back down to the Thai restaurant, because it was possible that the restaurant would close soon. I see the lady who just helped me. She is sitting with her daughter and group of friends. She smiles, and says she is pleased that my troubles got sorted out. I order a seafood curry and rice. It is a grand feast, a good end to the day.

Thank you to the ten or a dozen people who helped me to get to my destination today. People are kind and helpful, and I am grateful.

Strange lands and separation are the traveller's lot.

I Ching, 56, The Traveller, Richard Wilhelm

Chapter 9: Finding Cornwall in Ireland

I was still surprised by the frequency with which I was getting lost. I had trusted in the fact that I had Google Maps on my phone. I thought that this, combined with my long-held facility for mapping the terrain in my head, and thus finding my way around, would be adequate, so that getting lost should not have been a problem, or even necessitated much thought. But I got lost, so often.

Years ago, as young adults, my two daughters went overseas together: to England, Ireland and France. My eldest daughter told me her younger sister had an uncanny sense of direction in these foreign places. She gave me an example. They were in Paris, and had just travelled on the underground train, the subway. They were going to the Louvre. They came up the stairs out of the subway, and the younger one immediately said, "It's this way. Let's go," while the older one was standing there looking bewildered and directionless.

The older daughter said to me, "How did she know that? Neither of us had been there before. And I had no idea which way was which. Is it genetic?"

So I say to myself: "Is it genetic?" But I think, "Probably not."

Another theory: It's about being Antipodean. Because we come from the upside-down part of the world, we get mixed up about north and south (and therefore about east and west as well). So many times, I set off in exactly the opposite direction. The exactitude of it disturbed me. But I know this theory is frivolous, despite its lure.

I could also blame the weather. Very often, the sun was obscured by clouds, so the shadows were unclear and I was unsure which was east or west. I'm sure this theory carries some weight.

On this day in Waterford, I knew I would not get lost. I had reconnected with a lady I had known for a while in Sydney, fifteen years ago. She had gone back to Ireland, to Waterford, where she had been born. I still had contact details for her, and she was happy to meet up with me. She said she would show me around for a day.

She turned up in the morning in her car, across the road at the Three Shippes Inn. And off we went. She said she grew up near here, and went to school here. First, we went into town and went to the Bishop's Palace, which is now a museum. We had coffee, and while I was there, I booked into tours for tomorrow. She showed me the place where her grandfather started selling cars in Waterford, in the early 1900s. He was friends with Henry Ford, and Henry wanted him to come to America, but he wanted to stay in Ireland.

He made a lot of money. She told me that once there was a huge strike in the town (I don't remember the reason), and the strikers were surviving on small sums of money paid to them by the union. The problem was that the money was paid by cheque, and the banks were shut as part of the strike. So, her father cashed the cheques for strikers. The money was eventually paid back to him by the bank, so he didn't lose out, but he did a great service to people at the time.

He created great loyalty among people, and when they bought a car, they purchased it from him. She said that in her later life, her grandmother used to say that cars caused the decline of the smaller villages, because people would drive to the bigger town.

In the museum, there was a huge Waterford piece of crystal, about half a metre tall, standing on a pedestal close to a passageway: rather unprotected. Strange. We went across the road to the Waterford crystal place. It was an exhibition and sales centre. There were all sorts of glass: many pieces made as trophies for sport, cute things like a small aeroplane, a steam engine, etc. these pieces were made for sale, and the prices ranged from 1,000 to 40,000 Euro.

I suggested that the biggest market for these would be Americans. She agreed. Yes, that was it. There were traditional pieces too, like glasses and bowls: very exquisite and beautiful. There were also "modern" forays, such as glasses and bowls that featured black as well as clear glass. I didn't like them.

We decided to drive out into the country. We drove south (I knew that from having looked at places on a map), down to the coast. She said she had a house there, owned by herself and two siblings.

When we came to the coast it was cloudy, so the view was restricted. We stopped at a cove where there was a carpark. A couple of people were emerging from the water, to come back to a campervan. I suppose it is summer. Most of the beach was pebbles, but there was sand too. You could see the mountains in the distance, misty.

A little further on, to my surprise, we came across something I recognised from Cornwall: the remnants of mine workings. There was the square tower of the engine house, and the chimney. I said,

"Can we stop and look at this?" so we did. The sign said, "The Copper Coast, UNESCO World Heritage site". I didn't know there was copper mining in this part of Ireland. On my previous visit to Ireland, I had been shown the museum of a copper mine in Cork from the 1800s: Allihies.

The mine here dated from 1825 and went until around 1877. It was intensive, involving close to 2,000 miners at its peak. I discovered that most of the miners were from Cornwall. It is possible that I had people in my family who came here and worked in the mine. That was an exciting thought. The family forever becomes richer.

Now, there are maybe 200 people living in the vicinity. Many of the people who had been here migrated abroad, to America, Canada and other places. I took photos. Just after this, we came to a Church of Ireland that is now a heritage site featuring the mining. It was just across the road from my host's house.

My host's father bought the house when she was young, and the family used to come here in summer for beach holidays. She remembers what it was like as a child. They had their own well for fresh water. There were thirteen children in the family; she is number nine, with both brothers and sisters older and younger than herself. Most of them have died.

The house burned down about twenty years ago and it has been rebuilt. Some of the walls are from the original building, which was built in the 1800s. All the present windows come from a local manufacturer of windows, who supply many houses in this part of the world.

Later, when I bought a book about the local enterprise, she looked through it and found the house. It had been owned by the manager of the mine. There had been a copper mine here. On my father's side, many people had gone to Australia from Cornwall, and they had been miners of tin and copper.

She told me that when her father died, she didn't come, because she was living in Australia, but she heard many reports of the funeral. It was a huge event for the town, with a procession down the main street. Quietly, her father had given much support to the friary in town, and he used to go to mass most days before he went to work. He had donated to many causes without advertising the fact. This all became apparent at the funeral.

She said that one of her brothers did a eulogy, and at the end he started reciting the litany of the saints. She remembered that as s child: all the children used to have to kneel and pray while her father did the recitation, and they would be impatient, as kids are, but it was an important part of their life, and when her brother started the recitation, people around the church fell into weeping.

I went over the road to see the exhibit. There were a few people around, some sitting at the café. The exhibits included large posters of text and illustrations explaining what the mine was and its history, and its election to world heritage status recently. There were many exhibits of different types of rocks, for the geologically minded.

When I studied engineering briefly, after I had left school, we had to do a unit on geology, part of which was a test in identifying different types of rocks. I barely passed; it was a "Conceded Pass". I thought the meaning of this was, "We just want to get rid of you. Don't ever think about doing geology as a major subject." I accepted the verdict willingly.

However, I know some things, for example, basalt and sandstone, because I lived among them when I lived at Horseshoe Creek, Kyogle, but even so, there was a sample in the exhibition of sandstone and I didn't recognise it as such, not at all.

There was a section about a man from this area who studied earthquakes and how to measure them. There was a model of the mining site at Tankardstown, about two metres square. Towards the end of the exhibits, there was a section on notable people in the history of the district. One of them was a female writer, Una Troy (1910-1996), and a couple were artists. Not people that I'd heard of, but they had made a life here and attained local respect. You could immerse yourself in the landscape here.

In the museum there was a long bone, two metres, long. It was the rib of a whale that had washed up on the beach, dead, about fifty years ago.

Back in the café, I found some books for sale. And yes, I bought a book. It was a history of the mining in this area. Cornwall features in it, because Cornish people had the expertise that was needed. The author was Des Cowman. The title was *The Making and Breaking of a Mining Community*. It is interesting the way themes emerge in people's writing. The book has an index of names; I looked for the name Crosby but it is not there. However, the name Martin occurs. Some homework is required.

A wanderer with a purpose, is that how I need to think of you from now on?

Lana to Dane, *Wanderer,* Victor Kelleher

The next venture was to see a landed estate. There is one not far from here (here being Bunmahon). We drove down narrow winding roads and came to a gate. The gate was closed, but it had a sign on it about visitors. There was a man there on the inside, standing next to his car and a small gate lodge. My host talked to him. I couldn't make out a lot of it. Apparently he had a very broad Waterford accent.

The man had said that we could go through, but to go out the other end, because by the time we came back here, the gate would be closed. So we drove on a gravel road, a bit rough, but serviceable. At first it was grassy, but then we were in the middle of a forest, and we went over a couple of small bridges. It was a long time before we came upon any gates or buildings. The forest was taller. All of this was part of the estate, which was called Carraghmore.

In some places, the road was surrounded by a wide grassy verge. I wondered about what commercial activity the estate was involved in. I could see little, but I did wonder about how this forest measures up to the idea of wildness. In retrospect, I wonder about deer or other wild animals. We didn't see any.

After a couple of forks in the road, we came to a great building, surrounded by grass. We went through a gateway with tall ironwork gates, into an immense area like a parade ground. To the left and right were low buildings, looking like they had been the living quarters of servants and farm workers. Ahead was an immense house with turrets, obviously intended to be grand and imposing.

According to the sign, there are tours of the house during the day. We were too late for that, and there are tours of the garden, which is through a small gateway in the side building to the right. Apparently they hold a festival here once a year now. It sounds hippie-ish. We peeped into the garden. It is old; there are mature trees all around, and a very fine trimmed lawn in the middle. I imagine there is much more to it as you get in.

Along the wall between the house and the side buildings there are some alcoves with statues. Only two statues, but it looks as if there used to be more. The two statues were of pretty young women. To me they looked like classical Greek themes. They were lovely, if somewhat weather-worn.

We drove out towards where we imagined the gate was to get out. When we arrived, the gate looked shut, but I didn't have the feeling that we were locked in. When we got close, there was a man and a car and a small gate lodge. We were going to ask him about exiting, but when we were closer, the gate opened by itself. Magic. We asked the man about how to get where we needed to go next, and he said to take the lefthand road up over the hill until we got to a sharp lefthand fork.

It was a long way, and all the time we were driving, there was a high wall on our left. A lot of manual labour and expertise went into the building of this wall. The estate is huge, thinking in terms of miles in every direction. Long after we thought it was going to occur, we came to the sharp lefthand turn. The road was still very narrow, and occasionally a car came the other way and we had to stop and wait for it. But the road was sealed; no gravel now.

We stopped at a pub for dinner, a very old pub that has seen its ups and downs. Different people, I was told, have taken over and tried to make a go of it. But it was packed tight tonight, and it was loud. We went into a back room, which was quieter. The pub was called Tom Hayes on the inside, with a big sign, but outside it was called The Engine Room, because of the mining, I suppose.

We drove back to Waterford and parted ways. A very good day.

Chapter 10: Exploring Waterford

The weather was cold and windy: warm clothes needed. A few drops of rain early on, but none thereafter.

This was my day to explore Waterford, the city that used to be Ireland's biggest city, and at one stage was the capital of Ireland. Now it is what we would call a regional city. It used to be a major port, back in the day (say 1300s) when wine was a major import (from France, and later from Spain).

As I have so commonly done, I got lost on the way to town, and I still have trouble with Google Maps and compass directions. Sometimes it makes sense, and other times it seems back to front. What was probably a fifteen-minute walk took me forty-five minutes.

I was aiming for the Bishop's Palace, described as a Georgian grand house. It was lived in by the mayor for a long time. There was lots of Waterford crystal and other fine glassware on show. Some of the items were emotional pieces. Someone in New York commissioned a piece for the nine-eleven (2001) disaster. The artist focused on a miraculous recue in one of the stairwells of the first tower. It was quite moving.

There were also the drawings for an item presented to President Donald Trump in March 2017 for St Patrick's Day. This seems to be a traditional thing, and it was only a (bad) accident that Donald Trump was the president at the time. The tour was a reenactment by a short woman (shorter than me) acting as the housekeeper possessing secrets and gossip. The rooms contained large portraits of important people, all with dark surroundings. There was some nice furniture too.

With the different tours, some of the same stories turn up again, seen from a different perspective. After the tour, I went up to the top floor, which looked at life in modern times (1900s). This floor dealt with stories about Irish rebellion against the English, such as the Easter Uprising in 1916. There were stories from World War 1, such as the life of Irish soldiers in the trenches. There was a model of the vast extent of trenches and how men adapted to live in such abominable circumstances. And there were fragments of ordinary civil life.

The next organised activity I did was called the Epic Walking Tour of the Viking Triangle. The triangle is the small part of the city that was where the Vikings established themselves in Waterford around 900 AD. They turned up and settled; it wasn't really an invasion. Invasions occurred later when there were rival contenders to be king of all.

The tour guide said that Viking was a profession, not a race. Vikings killed and plundered. Then they might give up being a Viking and become a settler. The race was Norse. So, my Sarah Crosby could have had Norse blood in her (and therefore, so might I).

The guide showed us some surviving parts of the city wall, which had sections added to it over several hundred years. First it was wattle and daub, then it was stone.

He showed us a building that was flying the Irish flag: green, orange and white. Green was for Catholics, orange was for Protestants, and white was for the hope that they would live in peace. The flag flies all year. The building was where the Young Ireland movement housed itself, around 1848. The great leader was Thomas Richard Meagher. At the end of this street there was a statue of him on a horse, holding a sword high.

I have a story that fits in with this. Kevin O'Doherty was also in the Young Ireland movement, and he was arrested and initially sentenced to death (in 1848). This was commuted to lifetime exile and transportation to Van Diemen's Land. Meagher's story is the same. In his case, he escaped from Australia after a couple of years and went to New York.

The Irish rebels were different from the convicts. When they arrived, they were freed, on condition that they stayed within a designated area. Kevin O'Doherty's area was centred at the town of Oatlands, about halfway between Hobart and Launceston. A Roman Catholic man, John Ryan, invited Kevin to lodge in his house, called Elm Cottage. Until the local Roman Catholic church was built, Mass was said each Sunday in this house as well.

The relevance of Kevin O'Doherty is that he probably met Sarah Crosby in that house, at Mass. When Sarah arrived in Hobart, in April 1850, she was sent straight to Oatlands to work as a servant in one of the local inns, the Wilmott Arms. Sarah was Roman Catholic (she is buried in a Roman Catholic grave at Rookwood in Sydney;

she got married to Edward Lewis in a Roman Catholic church in Hobart), and it is likely that she went to Mass each Sunday. The inn where she worked was just across the road from Elm Cottage.

Was there anything romantic between Kevin O'Doherty and Sarah Crosby? I did explore the possibility, but eventually I had to conclude that it was unlikely. Part of the argument for this is that he was engaged to a lady back in Ireland, and a few years later, he did contrive to return and marry her. He was also ten years older than Sarah, and he was from the literate classes. Sarah, in contrast, was poor, from a farming background, and could neither read nor write. None of these reasons is conclusive, one might say, but sometimes the way it seems to be is the way it really is.

To return to the tour: we looked at a church that is being renovated. It is one of the earliest churches. There is not much more to it than a few walls. There is no roof. It belonged to the grey friars. I think they were Benedictine. There was a story about a churchman who died (maybe it was during a plague in the 1400s). He had said that he wanted to be buried near the Greyfriars church, but he was buried at another church nearby. A few years later, friends dug him up and reburied him, at night, in secret, where he had requested.

The story was that when the body was lifted, they could see that his body had not decomposed at all. The twelve-year-old boy who watched this, Luke Wadding, considered this to be a miracle, and the experience determined his way in life.

He grew up to become a scholar of the church. He lived in Rome for many years, assisting the Pope. He compiled a list of all the Irish saints, with their stories, the first person to do this. This included St Patrick, who was not known outside of Ireland at this time, and his birthdate was given as 17th March. Luke Wadding was the only Irishman who has been nominated for Pope.

St Patrick's Day was celebrated on 17th March as a public holiday from 1903.

The Bishop's Palace was designed by Richard Cassel in the 1740s, but the bishop died during its construction. A young man who had been an architectural assistant on the job, John Roberts, said he could finish the job, and he was given the responsibility for it. He went on to build two cathedrals in the city: both the Catholic and the Protestant. This is unusual. Roberts married the girl he wanted to, but both families opposed the marriage, and they ran way to London to elope. Subsequently they had many children, between twenty-one and twenty-four. Only eight survived to adulthood.

The house where he lived is said to be the "oldest urban house" in Waterford.

I saw a pair of statues: Strongbow and Aeofe, which is a modern representation of events in 1170. There was a problem with them marrying, because Strongbow was the Norman king, and Aeofe was the daughter of the King of Leinster. There was a battle, which Strongbow won, and twenty-four hours later, he and Aeofe married. But she died a year later. Some people in Ireland date the troubles with the English back to this time. For others, the problem is more recent, around the 1500s, with the plantations, and the granting of large pieces of land to English people.

My understanding of Irish history is undoubtedly still very muddled.

The traveller lives in the world, moving through it, not stuck or expecting fulfilment in external things.

I Ching, 56, Richard Rudd

I had lunch at O'Sullivans, a pub. When I walked in, they were playing Clannad: all the way to Ireland to hear this (I had been to a concert of theirs in Sydney). I had a fish pie and chips. It was nice. The man who greeted me said his son had come back from Australia (from Perth) yesterday.

The next tour I went on was the Medieval Museum. I spent some time here. I was the only person on the tour. It was interesting, although I could never remember all the historical events. It was a constant revolving door of wars, religious fights about theology, who was going to be the conqueror, and nasty business like King Henry VIII closing down all the monasteries because he wanted to cash in their treasures.

The museum had many treasures. Among them were some holy vestments worn by senior churchmen (bishops etc) on high occasions. The vestments were buried beneath the paving stones in the church so that the English king would not seize them. They remained buried for 150 years until they were discovered when the church was being rebuilt. They have gold thread in them, and they show scenes from the Bible.

The guide showed me one mystery. One of the robes has the manger scene from the Bible depicted on it: baby Jesus, Mary and Joseph and the three wise men (the magi). But when you look closely, another man is present, and he is unexplained. People say he looks like a first world war soldier. I am sure many minds have pondered over this. To say he looks like a first world war soldier is certainly imposing something on the garment. It is a mystery. Is it someone hoping for redemption?

There is a wine cellar, which belonged to the mayor of the city. Waterford had a legal monopoly on the importation of wine. However, ships often diverted to the town of New Ross, in Wexford, to avoid the tax on wine. At one point, the Waterford army went and destroyed New Ross.

The cellar has an arched roof. Some of it started as wattle-and-daub and was later made into stonework. The ceilings may have been smoothed over and painted. The wine was in casks.

There was a document on a scroll that is 2.5 metres long, that set out Waterford's claims, sent to the English king. Queen Elizabeth visited and saw it. She stood where I was standing, looking down at the glass case. Later, Prince Charles visited (when he was prince), and he stood on the same spot. He said, "Yes, mummy told me about this." There were photos in the case of each of them.

In the street outside, which is the square next to the cathedral, there is a large chess set, a replica of the Lewis chess set, which dates back to around 1100. It had been made somewhere in Europe, and a merchant was bringing it to Ireland to sell, but it ended up being buried on the island of Lewis in the Outer Hebrides of Scotland, where it remained for several hundred years. In 1831 it was discovered. Most of the pieces are now owned by the British Museum, and some are owned by the National Museum of Scotland and are in Edinburgh. It is the most famous chess set in the world.

I went into Christ Church Cathedral. There was a tour party there. I had been told there was a statue of a prominent person (1700s?). It was a cadaver statue, showing him in the state of decay, ribs sticking out. The great fear of people of the time was purgatory, the idea of being tortured for hundreds of years before getting to heaven. Thus the church offered indulgences, and rich people paid lots of money to the church. And you could get other people to pray for you. Theology meets commerce. The belief shaped all of society.

There was an organ playing in the church. Apparently, the organ has just been re-tuned.

There was a shop in the church, and I bought a cashmere scarf for my sister.

The last tour for the day was at the Irish Wake Museum. When I bought the ticket, I talked to the man at the desk. I told him about

Sarah Crosby, how she was born here, how she got to Australia, and how I found her grave at Rookwood. He was moved by the story.

The first part of the tour was about the history of the house, and about reclaiming it from disuse about twenty years ago and peeling back the layers of time.

The next part talked about plagues and medicine over time. And the last part talked about rituals around death. There was a model of an old woman lying in bed, dead. Rich people at funerals would have tokens (like coins or charms) made to give out to people.

I told the story to the group of how Sarah Crosby, in her will, requested that all of her grandchildren be dressed appropriately for her funeral (there were about fifteen of them). The tour guide said that she was probably remembering things from her childhood in Ireland.

All journeys have secret destinations of which the traveller is unaware.

Martin Buber

I thought it would be a good idea to have dinner, because I will be travelling tomorrow. I walked back into town via the river, which is just down the street from where I am staying. it's nice to have the feeling of water. I found a place, and ate a satisfactory dinner. Walking back, I saw a blue plaque on a nondescript building. It said that it was here that Thomas Meagher, the leader of the Young Ireland rebels, was arrested.

Chapter 11: Flying to Edinburgh

I vacated the unit and walked into town. The bus I had booked (JJ Kavanagh's) was leaving across the road from Dooley's Hotel. This is a bus station. But my bus to Dublin Airport did not show up on its screen. I had plenty of time, so no panic. I was sitting outside where the buses come, and an official came up and announced that a bus was cancelled, and we could try to catch Kavanagh's, which was across the road.

This was confusing, although I figured that the man was referring to a different bus being cancelled. However, it did tell me where the Kavanagh's bus was actually leaving from, and I was glad I had bought my ticket last night. The Kavanagh's bus did come, and there were indeed extra people. The bus driver was good-naturedly trying to accommodate whom he could, although he said he also had to pick up people down the road.

I hadn't realised it, but this bus was not going directly to the airport; it was stopping at many places along the way. It was also going into the centre of Dublin, which was very busy. At one town, he had to leave some people behind at the bus stop. So, the bus ride was very long, and we didn't get to the airport until 2:30 pm. I had allowed myself plenty of time today. Just as well.

Something happened on the bus. One of the extra people who got on at Waterford was a lady who was probably in her fifties. Her dress was worthy of comment: a bright yellow outfit with high-heeled black shoes: the kind of dress a woman would wear to a corporate event, especially if she were playing a hosting role in the event. She had blonde hair, and she had lipstick on. Her baggage consisted just of a small lady's handbag and a small paper bag, such as you might receive if you bought a small gift for someone.

She sat next to me. She was agitated, rocking backwards and forwards on her seat constantly. She spoke in snippets, some of which I didn't catch. I focused on exuding calm, creating a peaceful surround. After about half an hour she calmed down a little, and then volunteered more about herself. She was from Waterford, had lived there her whole life, and she had been an accountant. She retired last week.

Her troubles, she said, were to do with her husband, who mistreated her and had probably been unfaithful to her. This morning, she just walked out. She said she had to leave to sort her life out, and work out what she was going to do. She had no possessions with her except what I have recounted. She had no plan.

She was obviously not going to go overseas, because she did not have her passport with her. She got off at the airport and was asking someone about hotels. She obviously had enough money not to be desperate about money. Her name was Sharon.

I didn't say too much to her, I mean, I did not try to advise her. The main thing I said was that she should try to make a space for herself where she could be quiet and calm, because she would then be better able to make some good decisions. When she got off, I wished her well.

There are parallels between her and Sarah Crosby: both having to leave urgently, both having to leave people behind in a situation of distress, both having lived their whole lives in Waterford and then having to head out into the unknown, unprepared, not knowing where they are going.

I soon realised that no journey carries one far unless, as it extends into the world around us, it goes an equal distance into the world within.

Lillian Smith

The airport was the usual large-scale milling of people. I was one of the ones who were not sure what to do. However, I had downloaded the RyanAir app and so it was relatively smooth going, once I had asked an official for guidance. (You note my willingness to seek advice.) Then there was security. I had to take off my shoes as well as my belt. By the time I got through all the travel rituals, I was keen to have some food. It was about 3:00 pm and I hadn't eaten yet today.

I had a sandwich and an orange juice. It was very satisfactory. The flight went well. It was cloudy, but I saw some of the sea between Ireland and Scotland, and some of Edinburgh while we were coming in to land. I had thought to order a transfer, as we were coming in late in the afternoon, and I didn't want to be trying to find my way around and do a lot of the lost walking that I had been doing, and remembering my experience coming in to Waterford.

The car was a black Mercedes Benz taxi (eight seats) and a driver who used a lot of the back streets, given that it was peak hour. It took about forty minutes. The place I booked the other night is a block of flats geared towards students. I didn't mind that. My unit was on the sixth floor, which I also didn't mind, because it meant there would be a lift. I was looking forward to having a cup of tea.

There were several locked doors I had to go through, as the floor was divided into sections. When I got to the unit, it was quite modern, small but adequate. But there was no jug to boil water! And there were no cups, nor even a glass. There were plenty of power points and a student desk, but no way to make a cup of tea. The cost of a jug would only be about twenty pounds; in the great scheme of things, a miniscule amount.

66

Why no jug? Do students not have cups of tea or coffee? At the reception desk they told me you could purchase a cup of coffee for 2.75 pounds. To put it mildly, I was disappointed. This was worse than the Waterford unit, where I had to use the microwave to boil water. I thought about abandoning this place and finding a place that would have all of the fundamentals.

But, I am booked in for three nights, and to change such arrangements only ever means that you lose the money after a lot of aggravation. I needed to settle down and put things into context. I even thought about buying a jug and a cup: a bit later, I even saw a jug for sale in a shop window: 18.99 pounds. Just as I thought. And there were several charity shops around where I could have bought a cup.

However, I think I should do what any traveller would do: accept the conditions. I did acquire from the ground floor one of those fragile little plastic glasses you use to pour water into from a water dispenser.

It was 7:30 pm and I thought some dinner would be advisable. I walked down the street (Leith Walk), looking for places where I could eat. On the way, I came across three lads having a beer sitting on the outside tables of a pub. One of them was standing, watching me walk down the street. He greeted me (slightly swaying). I was receptive. He said, "You look mint." I asked him what that meant, and he said, "Walking down the street there, you look mint. You know, like mint condition." I had to smile at that; it was a nice compliment.

He told me that he was born in Edinburgh, but he now lived in Newcastle, but he had come back here for a short-term job. I told him that I left 150 years ago, and I went to Australia with my family. I came back too, for a look. We parted happily. He shook my hand.

There were numerous small bars, but I wanted a decent-looking, cheap place to eat. There were numerous ethnic choices. I ended up choosing Greek. The restaurant was occupied but not too crowded. The menu offered Mezes. The waiter recommended that I order two, and some pita bread. I ordered haloumi and portabella mushrooms and I thoroughly enjoyed it. I went back to the unit and did not have a cup of tea.

The unit does have a large window which looks north. I think that is the Firth of Forth that I can see from my window. Tomorrow I will explore Edinburgh, but I don't know what I will do for the rest of my trip. I have to go to Nottingham to see family, and I want to see Fife.

We wander for distraction, but we travel for fulfilment.

Hilaire Belloc

Chapter 12: Searching for ancestors in Edinburgh

My first day in Edinburgh. I walked, feet on the ground in my good walking shoes. My sense of direction? I am staying halfway down Leith Walk, a big main street, and I know that if I walk up the street, I will get to the centre of the city, and it does not feel as sprawling as Sydney is. What does it mean in terms of north, south, east and west? I am not sure. No, wait, the Firth of Forth is north of Edinburgh, so I should not despair. I am not entirely devoid of clues.

I thought I would check out where the building for Scotlands People is located. The records for family history (births, deaths and marriages) are there. The records go back to 1855, when civil records began in Scotland. They also hold many earlier records from church parishes. At home, if I am doing research into Scottish ancestors, I purchase a subscription and then conduct my searches on their website. I wonder what else the physical site may offer.

I walked up Leith Walk, which is so wide that it caters for cars, pedestrians, cyclists and trams, all of which have their own lanes. I found Scotlands People; it is located in the Registry Office. It was the first records office to be built in the UK, sometime back in the early 1800s,

I went in. There was a receptionist and then an inner room. The receptionist explained that I could book a desk for the day for fifteen pounds. But she said I won't see anything more than I have seen online at home. She was suggesting it would be a waste of time for me. But on the first floor there is a place that has legal and land records. I could pursue that. I thought about it, but I think the issues I am addressing would not be found in land or legal records (even though I think the records cover the places I am interested in, and the time frames).

I need to look at Census records for Ellen Welch's sponsors in Edinburgh: John Miller, William Goodsir, John Watson and Alexander Galloway.

I told the lady at reception that I was looking for a marriage in Edinburgh in 1748 that I had not yet been able to find, for Robert Bridges and Margaret Richy. Subsequently they went to the parish of St Leonards and St Andrews (near the city of St Andrews) to live. The parish council called Robert and Margaret into a meeting, and accused them of living in sin because they had not been married in the parish. But Robert went prepared; he took with him a document which stated that they had been married in Edinburgh on 8 April 1748 by the Reverend William Jamison.

I wondered if could explore the church records for Edinburgh, despite the fact that I don't know which church it was. However, the lady told me I was unlikely to find the marriage, because it was not obligatory to register marriages. I am wary of disappearing down blind alleys, so I thought I would leave it.

I went into the exhibition. It was in a round room. All the walls were lined with books, which are land records, called Sisenes. The room was domed, very high. When I looked up, the dome was very beautiful, pale yellow with white plaster rosettes. It looked brand new. I asked the attendant, and she said it was cleaned only three years ago.

Outside the building, a man in a kilt was playing the bagpipes. It seems that someone is playing bagpipes all day all over the city. While I was there, a group of Japanese tourists were using the bagpipe player as a prop for their photographic poses. He played on, impassive.

I went into a nearby café and had a coffee and croissant. Then I found a bus tours place. I chose a tour of the city. This will show me the scope of the territory. I booked a ticket. It was a clever strategy to avoid getting lost.

I had time, so I walked up a set of stairs and found a cemetery. This is part of Calton Hill. Most of the graves go back to the 1700s and 1800s. There was a monument to Abraham Lincoln for Scottish soldiers who fought in the Civil War. One more thing I didn't know.

There were many small alcoves. They looked like lockable cells, but they usually had plaques around the walls, and often a cap or spire or obelisk on top. There was one for David Hume, the philosopher. There was some kind of battlement around the cemetery as well. I wasn't expecting to find any ancestors here. As far as I know, all my ancestors lived in the country, not the city.

After this, I walked further up the street and saw that the street went up to the top of Calton Hill. There was an observatory up there in the 1800s. The astronomer had been an astronomer in South Africa in 1832. The view from the top is great; you can see towards all four directions around the city, and you can see Fife across the Firth of Forth (which used to be called the Frith of Forth in the 1790s, according to the panorama in the Registry Office).

There was also a stand of six columns which is a National Monument. They were free-standing, just a spectacle on their own. They might have been twenty metres high. It didn't make much sense to me, but it was imposing.

The bus tour was on the classic double-decker with half of the top roof removed. I sat upstairs. I thought I would be able to take photos, but it's too hard. Either the bus is moving, or the angle is wrong, or there is something in the way. Oh well.

I can't remember everything we saw, or what the man said, although much of it was rubbish. He must have mentioned Sean Connery a dozen times, and about a hundred places to shop. But it was my first survey of the extent of the city, and it gave me some ideas for places to come back to and visit. I also saw Niddry Street, which is where Sarah Blasko (a singer from Australia) will be playing on 1st July. I have a ticket for the show, which I bought in Sydney before I left.

In the Princes Street Gardens, I booked onto a tour at the Scott Monument, which is an extraordinary monument to the author. I had time for lunch, so I went over the road to Marks & Spenser's Foodhall. So, I can say I have shopped at Marks & Spenser's. I bought a salad with potato and salmon (a not-surprisingly rather small portion of salmon).

I also walked to the National Portrait Gallery, although I was more interested in the toilet than the portraits. Maybe I will come back.

And I walked further down the park, where there was another statue. The Scots certainly had many great men, or at least, they felt the need to commemorate many important men. I wanted to see a statue of Robert Louis Stevenson, because I had bought a book of his at a Sydney book fair. It wasn't one of his most famous novels; it was called *St Ives*.

However, the statue I was looking at was obscured by bushes. You couldn't get close enough to read a name, and it wasn't on Google Maps because it was right next to a floral clock, which was. While I was waiting in the park, a girl turned up and settled down to sing. It was nice, like a young Sarah Blasko. Later in the day, when I was walking along the Royal Mile, I saw her again; she had transferred herself to there.

The tour of Walter Scott's monument was up a spiral staircase to lookout points, just over 200 steps up, in three flights. The stonework was extremely ornate, and the style feels different to Oxford or Bath or London. I have photos. I think it's incredible that there is such a monument to a writer, especially a writer of novels, not a philosopher or scientist. But, one of the statements in the exhibits at the first stage said he had done more for Scotland than anyone. That is a bold statement.

Scott wrote the novels *Ivanhoe* and *Waverley*.

I said it before, but after seeing all the stonework I've seen over the last ten days, it's incredible to me that Charles Eaglestone and his ancestors were stonemasons. What they could have worked on!

The view from the highest level they took us to was grand. There wasn't much space to move around, but you could get to all the compass directions and see distance. I could see Fife, and the Royal Castle. Balmoral Hotel was in front of us. Famously, the clock is five minutes fast. It is near a railway station, and it allowed you five minutes extra to make the train. An engineer comes at Christmas to change it to the right time, and it stays that way until 2nd January, so that New Year is the same time as everywhere else in the time zone.

Man is so made that all his true delight arises from the contemplation of mystery, and save by his own frantic and invincible folly, mystery is never taken from him; it rises within his soul, a well of joy unending.

Arthur Machen

(This is the epigram on the title page of an anthology of detective stories, *Great Short Stories of Detection, Mystery and Horror*, 1928, edited by Dorothy Sayer.)

I walked down the stairs to Waverley Station, to use the toilet. There was a toilet in the shopping centre down there, but it had a turnstile, and people were using a token or a coin to enter. I don't know where to start with that. This tradition died out in Sydney when I was still a boy. What I remember from my childhood is a female attendant being in the foyer of the female toilet, in the city. This didn't happen in the men's, just the women's. I think women were expected to pay a token amount of money to this attendant. What services did she provide? Did she see that the ladies' dresses and hats sat right as they exited?

I thought I would see what the Scottish Storytelling Centre was about. The map (a paper one I had obtained from the Airbnb place) said it was next to New College. The latter houses the School of Divinity of the University of Scotland. You can walk into a courtyard and look around, and that's that. It was a nice square, and it had views of a church steeple which was somewhere further away and higher up.

The maps do not tell you that you are walking up a steep hill. There is a steep hill in the street where New College is. It is an effort to proceed. One does not expect miracles from maps, but one needs to take into account that a road that looks quite flat on the map may in fact be steep, perhaps even rather steep.

As to the Storytelling Centre, there was no place that could have been it. Not at all. One expects maps to be correct. Now I don't think that is always true. I think the same might be said of Google Maps on occasion (but which occasion?). Sometimes I think the maps are just wrong. Is this yet another factor which might help to explain my lostness? I wish it were that simple.

So, I walked up the hill and then suddenly I was in the middle of the Royal Mile. The Royal Mile runs between Edinburgh Castle and Holyrood Palace, the royal palace in Scotland. There are two things to be said about it: first, all the tourists come here, and second, it leads up to the Royal Castle. I walked up for a while. I passed a sign that said, "Sold out for today", and a portable stadium that was being erected, with probably over a thousand seats. A show must be coming up. Is it the Royal Tattoo?

Walking back down, the large spire that I had seen from New College turned out to be, not a church, but an ex-church. There were signs advertising an Edinburgh Festival. Was it the Fringe Festival? I do not know, and since I am only here now, and not then, it hardly matters.

Along the Royal Mile, there are all the tourist gift shops whose names I have heard. I went into one shop, which sold scarves and other items in tartans. The scarves were nice, but a Chinese shop assistant was shadowing me and she was determined. They had cashmere and other blends, all very nice. I didn't buy anything. Also, I didn't see any reference to which tartans they were. I thought that was odd. And further, I did not see the Mackie tartan.

Near to the huge no-longer-church there was a smaller church that was open: St Columba's. People were going in. It was a church that was still active, and the tourist season was an opportunity to save souls. It had tracts aplenty. Inside the church was an exhibition of the history of Christianity, and of religion in Scotland. It depicted the Picts as Christians, whereas I thought they were of a very old religion, about which not a lot was known. On posters over two metres high it spelled out the fortitude of Christianity through the Reformation, the assaults of philosophers and scientists and so on. I think their bias was showing.

And I was confronted by a man who wanted to weigh me up for conversion. He asked me if I had any beliefs. I said I didn't focus on beliefs, because that just leads to arguments (meaning, my beliefs are better than yours). I was being provocative, because the man wanted to give me answers. I knew they would be prescriptive, judgemental and, most of all, exclusive. You would only believe something different if you wanted to go to Hell. He wanted to pray for me. I said he was welcome to do that.

I kept it tight. If I had told him anything about what I believe or do, the war would have been on. He had certainty, and he wanted to offer it to me. I was part of his lost folk who must be looking for a shepherd, but in this context, I had my bearings.

Down the street I went into another church: St Giles. It was imposing: so many columns, so high, so many monuments and testimonials, and stained glass. In one section there was a display about archaeological work on the church environs, and what DNA is telling us. I didn't stay for the answer to that, but I did find a bronze statue of Robert Louis Stevenson. It was larger than life, with the man reclining and obviously pondering what he was going to write next. Or, perhaps he was pondering where to go next.

For my part, I travel not to go anywhere, but to go. I travel for travel's sake. The great affair is to move.

Robert Louis Stevenson

On the way back, I stopped at a little cart outside a new shopping centre to get felafels, which are always nice. And two doors up from where I am staying, there is a yoga studio: called Tribe Yoga. Someone was there, so I went in to chat. I told her about my yoga classes in Sydney. She said they have a couple of yoga studio sites. This one has been open since 2016. I don't think I will go for yoga. It would be too disruptive for them; they can only see things in terms of new members. I am not a new member; I am an itinerant, a traveller, merely a visitor.

So, that was my day. Now I have to think about where I am going to go after I leave here. The girl in the yoga place said the trains are good for getting to Fife. I was thinking I might have to hire a car. It might still be necessary, but we will see. I did think to acquire an International Driver's Licence before I left Sydney.

Chapter 13: Bookshops in Edinburgh

This was Day 2 of seeing Edinburgh. I started off with a different way of being lost.

I had to find out what was happening with my phone. I got a message saying I had used up all my data. I found the Vodaphone shop in Princes Street. The boy who talked to me said I could sort it out online. But, I said, I was here and perhaps he could help me. Many aspects of modern life are not nice, and young people don't seem to know what's at stake. They feel compelled to trust in the machine. Unfortunately.

I explained that I had been in Ireland for a few days. He said that might explain it: you have less data available to you in Ireland. I wondered what that meant. He said I only need to start worrying if my data use becomes locked. And it's true, I would worry then. It was all so vague, and I had the suspicion he didn't understand what he was talking about, and that this is par for the course. So that was that.

Whether or not one is lost is a question of clarity.

One of my missions today was to find an Edinburgh bookshop or two, and see if the I Ching was recognised. But I had already found one shop, just up the street from where I am staying: Topping & Company, the bookstore I had found in Bath. I do like the feel of their stores, although a) I am not interested much in fiction, and b) there are too many books, far more than I could ever read.

There were no I Ching books. There were a couple on the Tao Te Ching. I saw one book I thought was interesting, and the book was small enough to carry. It was a philosophy of the home, by Emanuele Coccia, translated from the Italian. I had always thought there should be such a book. I had not heard of the author, but given that he is Italian, that may not be surprising. Do lost travellers have a philosophy of home? It seems to be the necessary counterpoint.

On the way to find Blackwells, I got lost and walked here and there, to different parts of the city that I had not seen. I saw the building for National Records (this is different to the one I saw yesterday). It's a nice old building: imposing, secure. The streets were quieter and wider.

I found St Mary's Catholic Church (not intentionally), which was as grand as anything I've seen over the last few days. It was also the quietest. There were three or four people around, but the place was silent. It had a big organ: big pipes. The ceiling was very tall, and there were many stained-glass windows. The place had many small alcoves, each for 5-30 people, so you could have a small, personal service, despite the vast size of the building.

I did find Blackwells, near to the University of Edinburgh. It was similar to the shop in Oxford in feel. There were three floors, with sections for fiction, children's books, British history, sci-fi, etc, and sections for Religion and Philosophy. The result? I found one book on the I Ching, Richard Wilhelm's book, republished recently with fuzzy text, just like the one I had found in Dymocks in Sydney. (I told this story in *A Singular Book of Great Esteem.*) There were a few books on the Tao Te Ching, and that was it. I did not buy any books. I had a vegetarian roll and a cup of tea at their cafe. How good the tea was!

I walked again, just up the road to the National Museum of Scotland. It was about three o'clock, so I had two hours, by which time one's head has had enough anyway. It started with some ancient pieces: a large Buddha, an Egyptian statue, a cast iron fretwork pagoda with birdbath (which was made for the Grand Exhibition in 1888 in London) and a huge wooden bowl which I thought was a boat. It was not; it was for holding food to serve at a banquet. It came from the Cook Islands around 1841. One wonders how this eventuated.... it must have been prized. It was made from a single piece of wood, that is, carved from one tree.

There was a technological section, with a very early steam engine (1820s). From James Watt, who we now learn was involved in the slave trade. There were some small aeroplanes, and an old car, an Argyll, very jaunty in red.

There was a section on religion and politics: this is a vast slice of Scottish life. And there was a section on the evolution of industry from crafts. There were some weaving machines, and also an explanation of how cloth was woven in the days before machinery, using water wheels. I copied some of the explanatory texts. There were holy artefacts from the various churches.

This section probably contains the explanation of why the Mackie family left Scotland in the 1850s. Alexander was a weaver (1851 Census).

There were some modern artefacts, for example, a succession of telephones from the early days through to modern times. I recognised some styles from through my lifetime. There were some motorbikes, and bicycles, including penny-farthings.

I am going to Nottingham next, to visit family, so I had to organise my trip south. I decided this was an opportunity to go to Durham. I will get the train to Durham and spend two nights there before I get another train to Nottingham.

Chapter 14: The writers of Scotland

I am moving today, because I want something other than "student accommodation". The shower is so tiny you can hardly turn around. I asked again about tea at reception: I thought they might have hot water for tea. But you have to pay 2.75 pounds anyway, and I checked and there are no tea bags. Obviously, students drink coffee if they drink anything hot at all. But I asked reception if I could leave my suitcase here tomorrow until 3:00 pm, and that is okay.

The new place is a further ten minutes' walk down the road, away from the city. It's in a side street off the main road. On the corner there is another lovely stone church, built in 1861. So, when my Scottish ancestors moved to Australia, this church hadn't been built yet. I found that interesting.

I got lost, a little bit: I got the number of the place wrong, and I turned up at number 19, instead of where I should have been. A man answered the door. He could see I was looking for a place of accommodation, and he said this place was not it and nor had it ever been.

My problem was that I could not see the screen of the phone clearly in the sun, so I couldn't check my Gmail messages. And when I could, I went through three messages and could not see the actual address. There is a constant onslaught of selling that you have to wade through as well. The man was polite but a bit annoyed. Anyway, I eventually found the address and made my way back.

Once I had arrived at the correct place, I couldn't find the message which had the instructions for getting in. I ended up sending a message to the host (having found how to do that). However, in the meantime, I found the number I had to key into the panel beside the door. It was 1969. That was amusing, because I could find many stories to go with that. It was the year that The Rolling Stones appeared at Altamont and hired the Hell's Angels motorcycle gang as security, and there was (foreseeable) violence in which six people died.

Also, yesterday when I had been at Blackwells, I wanted to use the toilet, and you had to ask at the café for a code. The code was 1492, the year that Columbus discovered America. Probably other things happened that year as well.

My room is at the top of the stairs on level one. There are twenty-four stairs. That is the price of high ceilings. This is an old house.

I was standing at the traffic lights this morning, in front of the Registry Building where Scotlands People is. A family was standing next to me. The girl, who was about three, pointed at the building and asked her mother, "Is that an old building?" I thought that was beautiful.

There's a whole world there: the concepts in a child's mind and how they are formed, what experiences the child has had, and the distinctions they are making, and it is always evolving. The irony is that almost all the buildings are old.

This morning, I registered online as a member of the National Library of Scotland, because you need a reader's card to be in there.

I thought I should start putting my presence here to good use. But on my way there I saw Niddry Lane, and I thought I should use the opportunity to locate The Cave, where Sarah Blasko is playing on 1 June.

There are two blocks to the street. It is narrow and cobble-stoned, with old buildings all the way down. I found the place. On its left-hand side, a sculpture of a black and white cow is leaping out of the building, just the front end of it. On the right-hand side, the same cow is diving into the building, so you can see just the rear end of it. Just so you don't mistake which place it is. It's about thirty minutes' walk from where I am staying now, and I don't think I will get lost.

I still wanted to go to the library, but I thought that coffee and a bite to eat would be good. The café was called Blank Street. It was on a very busy street which was very popular with tourists. There were plenty of shops to buy Scottish tartans et cetera. Princes Street. The statue in the nearby square was of King George IV. Subsequently I realised that this was close to the Writers' Museum, but Edinburgh has streets that seem to defy Google Maps' limited logic.

I walked around for forty minutes in large circles trying to find it. There were several problems. Some streets are way above others. You can be in a street and high above you is another street, which is a main road, and there is no connection between the two. There are also tiny passages between streets and up and down the hills, so there are lots of stairways. Google Maps doesn't reflect any of this. So, I have seen a lot more of Edinburgh, and now I recognise many things, but I still can't piece much of it together.

The relevant image is one that I saw in Herne Hill: the pieces of a jigsaw scattered on the ground. The pieces are there, but I don't know the relationships between them.

In the end, Google Maps said to go around the block. The problem was that a whole street was closed for construction work. You can get through, between barricades and workmen, but it looked problematic. Then I saw a hole in the wall, saying Lady Stair's Close. That rang a bell, and I went in.

Wikipedia lists all the closes in Edinburgh. What is a close? "Edinburgh's closes are narrow, historic alleyways that branch off the Royal Mile, offering glimpses into the city's past. Many were named after prominent residents or trades that operated within them. They served as residential access routes, workspaces, and even social hubs. Today, they remain a key part of Edinburgh's historic character and a popular attraction for visitors."

One may still be lost, but nevertheless culturally attuned.

I came out in a courtyard, surrounded by six-storey old buildings, all built in the 1600s and 1700s. Close to me was the building that houses the Writers' Museum. I had arrived. It was a three-storey building with round turrets in the corners. It commemorated three writers: Robert Burns, Sir Walter Scott, and Robert Louis Stevenson. There were three levels that visitors can explore, one for each of the writers.

There were busts of the three men. They are much-loved Scottish writers. Perhaps Burns is the most loved, the man as well as his poems, but Scott is the most revered, Fittingly, there was a model of the spire that I visited yesterday. It is about three metres tall, beautifully rendered. There were also photos of its construction. And the exhibition of Stevenson's life was in the basement of the building. He came a bit later in time, and he is the greatest adventure novelist.

The exhibition was saying that these three men created Scotland's sense of itself as a distinctive, cohesive people. I thought Stevenson's life was the most interesting. He was the traveller who went all over the world, and settled in Samoa. He liked the life there, and that is where he died. As a settler in a new place, he never lost his sense of Scotland, his birthplace.

I guess I relate to Stevenson more because of my encounter with one of his books, the one I had found at a book fair in Sydney. It was an old hardback book, published in about 1928. It was called *St Ives*, and I bought it because I thought it was about the town of St Ives in Cornwall, and many of the Martin ancestors emigrated from there to Australia.

But that was not what the book was about. St Ives was the name of a French person. The story is about a French soldier who was captured in the Napoleonic wars (probably about 1810?) and who was imprisoned with his comrades in Edinburgh Castle. He escaped from there and travelled through England. There was also a love affair with a woman from Edinburgh.

The book was engaging to me because I generally read little fiction. Once I realised what the book was about, I could have stopped there, but I followed the story right through to the end. At this point I discovered that Stevenson had died (in Samoa) before he finished the book. There was only a chapter or two to go, and the publisher enlisted the talents of Sir Arthur Quiller-Couch to complete the story. Steevenson's stepdaughter had been serving as his secretary during his last days, and had been writing the story down as he dictated it to her.

So, the book was famous for that, and there was text on the posters at the museum to say so. And I would not have known any of this had I not picked up the book at the book fair.

The building had very narrow spiral staircases going from floor to floor. None of the writers had any connection to the house. There was a little shop, and I bought a little book: by Stevenson, *A Child's Garden of Verses*. I think I already have a copy at home, but this one will have come from the Writers' Museum. [Later: I did not find the book in my collection.]

I had some lunch in the square. Several groups of tourists passed through, often with leaders who spoke other languages: German, Dutch, French, from what I could gather. I have heard a lot of Irish accents in Edinburgh too. Most of the Scots I can understand, but then, this is not the Highlands. When I had a cup of tea later at the National Library, the girl on the counter was Australian, from Melbourne. She could hear that I was Australian, and she dropped some Australian expressions on me using a broad Australian accent. I think she did it deliberately, just to enjoy the experience of it. I enjoyed it too.

So now we come to the work of the day. The first library I went into, I discovered, was the City Library of Edinburgh, not the National Library. The latter was across the road. Nevertheless, the young man listened to my story about Ellen Welch, and my wanting to know more about the migration scheme under which she came to Australia. He pointed me to a shelf of books, which were all about the Scots emigrating, mostly to America and Canada, but also to Australia.

The most relevant book was published by the University of NSW Press. I should be able to find it in Sydney. It covered the period of migration from 1830 to 1880 or so. Mostly it was interested in the emigration of tradesmen, but there was mention of women as well. And there was mention of John Dunmore Lang and his efforts to bring Presbyterianism to the rough colonial world.

See Malcolm Prentis, *The Scots in Australia* (I may have this book; if so, I thought it was of limited use). [Later: I found this book on my shelves; I have read it.]

From there I went over the road to the National Library, and I received my Reader's Card, complete with my photo. I explained to a library lady what my quest was. She said their whole Family History section had just been refreshed, and I could browse there. I spent an hour browsing through what was on offer. There were some serious books there, very high-level, academic. But there were several books that took my interest.

There was a book called *Tracing your coal-mining ancestors*. One gets easily distracted.

One book: *A History of Everyday Life in Scotland*, 1800-1900, edited by Trevor Griffiths and Graeme Morton. This book was another diversion from the life of Ellen Welch. It throws light on the disciplining of the congregation by the church between 1750 and 1850. Very relevant to the Bridges romance story. I copied the pages.

The relevant chapter was Chapter 3 by Andrew Blaikie: "Rituals, Transitions and Life Courses in an Era of Social Transformation."

The librarian suggested I look at the newspapers, but I didn't want to do that today; that could take a full day in itself. Perhaps another day. I don't leave until Wednesday.

Weather: there was a threat of rain this morning, and the sky got darker, but no rain eventuated. It was a warmish day. I could wear my coat without sweltering, which is good because it holds my wallet and my phone. At the National Museum yesterday there was a weathervane, and a story. It is thought that the word 'weather' relates to wind in particular. The wind brings the weather.

I walked back to the first Airbnb and picked up my bags, and walked down to the new place.

This is better than where I was before. It has a good amount of space, and there is a kettle so I can make tea. It is in a quiet area; the view is down onto a quiet suburban street. But the main road is close by.

Things I am remembering: the antlers of deer. At the Medieval Museum in Waterford was a set of a giant deer's antlers that are about 12,000 years old. They were found in Wexford in 1943. They are the largest known (apparently there is also a set at the UK Grant Museum). The antlers are about three metres across. It is a full set, unbroken. They were recovered from ice, I think. They weigh around

45 kilograms. They grow in a season and then fall off the stags each year, and they regrow for the next season. At the National Museum of Scotland yesterday, there was a full skeleton of a giant deer, together with the antlers.

In the book I am reading, *Wild Once* by Vivienne Crowley, I am just reading the chapter about deer as the manifestation of our bond with natural power.

Chapter 15: Libraries and bookshops

This morning it is raining lightly. Up to now it has been fine. I was thinking about going to the National Library again, and I am looking at the tram service on a flyer. Perhaps I should initiate myself. I have to think about how to organise the Fife part of my journey too.

Given the mildly inclement weather, I decided on a tram ticket for five days, at a cost of fifteen pounds. The tram stop is at Balfour Street, which is nearby, and it gets me to Princes Street, which is not far from the library.

It was rainy most of the day, although not heavily.

It was a good day to go to the National Library. I got the tram. They have a conductor who checks tickets. I had the QR code on my phone and that was fine. I have learned some things! There is space for luggage on the tram, so I can use it on Wednesday to get to the rail station (Waverley).

At the library, first, I made decent copies of the pages I found yesterday on social life in Scotland in the 1700s and 1800s.

Next, I got a computer and accessed the British Newspaper archives. I know I could do this at home, but I am in Scotland, and I am doing it here. I was looking for advertisements of emigration schemes around 1840. I wasn't exactly successful, but I can paint a picture of the times, and the different forces that were around, including people's experiences and opinions.

I also found other things related to people in my family tree, such as the Young Irelanders.

I was upstairs on the mezzanine level. There were only a few others around. Then I thought I heard snoring, and a guard turned up. She tried to persuade the snoring person to move on, and he said, "Just let me finish my work", which was amusing, given that he had been asleep. After a few minutes, he did move on.

By 2:30 pm I had had enough. I had lunch downstairs because it's probably cheaper here than in Tourist Town. It was a nice vegetarian roll and salad. Outside, it wasn't quite raining, but it wasn't quite not raining either. The streets were packed with tourists. At the City Hall, which has a square in front and a statue of a horse in the middle of the square, there was a bride and groom and several bridesmaids, all dressed up and happy and having their photos taken.

I walked down South Bridge Road to Princes Street, to the Register Building. Still crowded. This time, there were a bride and groom walking up the street among the crowd, and following them were about a hundred people all dressed up, men and women. Is this marriage in Edinburgh, on a Saturday afternoon? It was all very jovial.

I walked down Leith Walk, all the way down the hill. I wanted to visit some bookshops that I had seen. McNaughton's, also called Typewrongers, was the first. The left-hand section was old books, and the right-hand section was current books. In the old-books section, the predominant feeling was geography: books about places. There were also literary books, and poetry. Many of the books looked well over a hundred years old. Moreover, they looked as if they had been sitting on these shelves for a hundred years.

There was one book of poetry whose author I knew: Miroslav Holub. I had bought one of his books in the early 1970s, as a young man, and I liked it. [Later: I found the book in my collection; it was published in 1967.] His poems were mostly quirky little pieces; he had an interesting mind. The book in the shop was bigger. I did not buy any books.

Further down the road there was a second-hand store that had a separate books section. The shop was called Bethany. I'm sure it is a charity. I perused but did not buy. Closer to where I am staying, there was a bookshop called Elvis Shakespeare. It sold music (records and CDs) as well as books. I inspected the merchandise but did not feel compelled to buy.

It was actively drizzling now, so I thought I should buy some food to take back to the flat. In their wisdom, the managers of the flats have provided one fork and one teaspoon. I found a Turkish shop and I bought a fetta and spinach snail, and four small baclava. I had dreamed about the latter yesterday.

The food was excellent. The lady in the shop came from Brazil, but she said the people who owned the shop were Turkish.

I organised the material that I obtained today. There are two more places I can investigate for family history. One of them is Family Search (the Mormons), and the other is the Scottish Genealogy Society. That's for Monday. Tomorrow I might go and see the Falkirk Wheel.

I remembered this: a tee shirt from yesterday. The wearer: a teenage Chinese girl. Said tee shirt was red. It said: "Maybe today, Satan". I thought that was clever, turning the tables on Satan, trying to rope him in instead of the other way round.

And Brian Wilson from The Beachboys died the other day. He found expression for pure joy, unburdened, in amongst the troubles of his life.

Life is movement, and movement cannot be stopped. One should neither fear to move nor lose the stillness within.

I Ching, 56, Hua-Ching Ni

Chapter 16: A visit to the Falkirk Wheel

Another day. I got the tram to St Andrew's Square, and found my way to the rail station (Edinburgh Waverley: the only station in the world to be named after a novel). I want to go to the Falkirk Wheel. I also want to see what things are like for Wednesday, when I leave Edinburgh and get the train to Durham. It's a big station, like Central, and it's rather a maze.

I solved the puzzle on the way back in the afternoon. If I get out of the tram at St Andrew's Square and walk down to Princes Street, I go left and cross the road at Barclay's Bank. Then, on the street level, there is a lift that goes right down to the platforms.

I wanted to buy a ticket at a ticket office, not buy it from a machine. There are plenty of ticket machines, but to buy a ticket from a person, you have to go all the way back out to the street to find the office. I did find the office. The lady at the counter was strikingly beautiful, blonde, and she spoke with a Russian accent. I am not making this up.

I purchased a return ticket to Falkirk Grahamton. I was handed paper tickets, one for outgoing and one for return. I went backwards and forwards a few times to try to find Platform 13, but I am sure it would all make sense after a week. The train was standing at the platform, ready to leave in twenty minutes' time.

It was a nice run westward, five stations to my destination. Several small communities along the railway line, all inhabited now by commuters, I suppose. At one point I could see the towers and cables of the new bridge over the Firth of Forth to Fife. There were fields, and I saw one enormous barn, for pigs, I presume. I saw one horse and several cows.

I said it was sunny this morning. It is not; it is overcast, although it did not rain all day. It was a little chilly, but I am sure not like winter cold would be here.

The train was crowded, mostly Scottish people but including some Texan Americans. The journey was only about forty minutes. I alighted and tried to get Google Maps to direct me to a bus stop and to a bus. But the type was too small and the screen too glary: useless. I had gleaned previously that the bus stop was at St Andrew's church, so I just looked for a steeple. I soon found it and walked towards it.

I asked one bus driver, and he said he was going the opposite way. I didn't take that badly; I didn't know what direction the Falkirk wheel was from the station. This was not an instance of north-south-east-west confusion.

I crossed the road. I asked three people about a bus toward the Falkirk Wheel and got three different answers, one of which I didn't understand (an old man with a thick Scottish accent). I asked a girl, but she seemed vague about it.

I asked another bus driver, and he said I wanted the bus in front of him, so I skipped a bit and hurried, and got that bus (Number One) just as it was leaving. I bought a return ticket. The funny thing was that the girl was on this bus; she got off before I did, and then in the afternoon, she got on the same bus as me to come back to the rail station. Did she remember what she had said to me, or that she had contributed to my momentary lostness, or was she embarrassed?

Mingle with others as a stranger whose identity and mission come from a distant centre.

I Ching, 56, Stephen Karcher

The bus driver let me off at a big roundabout, where the Boardwalk Restaurant was situated. It is closed for renovations. The walk to the Falkirk Wheel from there was about fifteen minutes. I was the only one walking. There were not many cars either, although the car parks were huge.

There was low forest on both sides of the road. I passed a stile that you could step up onto to get through the fence into the forest. I could tell it had not been used for a while, because it was entirely overgrown. There were a few cyclists on the road, and twice as many dog walkers.

I reached the bank of a canal, a stretch of water that was maybe ten metres across, just enough for two boats to pass. I walked a bit further, then I could see the giant structure. It is the most preposterous thing, combined with great imagination and advanced engineering finesse.

At one stage I saw a pair of white swans with six young, half-grown and still soft grey in colour: cygnets.

I watched the wheel for a while. It went through a cycle where it took one boat up and another boat down in its two buckets. It takes about five minutes, with the whole apparatus moving slowly. It's about forty metres high, turning on a central axis. The boat coming down was full of passengers. When the machine stopped, the boat moved forward into the lagoon and edged its way towards the edge, where the people got off and the boat moored.

You can buy tickets to do this, but I am happy to watch; not much purpose would be served by going up and down. I watched the next iteration of the movement. This time, the boat coming down had just four people and a dog onboard. They looked as if they might be living on the boat. When they reached the bottom, they moved forward into a lock. Two men onshore were working the arms of the lock. When the boat was settled, the water in the lock flowed out and the boat gradually descended. When it settled at this level, the gate opened and the boat moved forward out of the lock. It had two choices now: to go left or right. It went to the right, and the little family went on its way.

That was satisfying, to see the process at work. It is what I had come for. Now I climbed the hill to the top canal. I walked along it, and it went into a tunnel which was 200 metres long. At the other end it veered left and continued. I came back and walked along another track which said it went to an old Roman wall and fort. There was forest and a few branching tracks. I gave up trying to find the Roman fort and returned to the wheel and the buildings.

I decided to return to Edinburgh, as I had achieved my objective, and I wasn't sure if it would rain. I walked back to a bus stop and waited ten minutes. Then it was a smooth journey back to the place where I was staying. I think tonight I will seek out the Vietnamese restaurant that is down the road, on Leith Walk.

That was a "good enough" day: satisfying, satisfactory.

I went down the street for dinner. I ended up at a Punjabi place. Dinner was lovely. It was a cash-only place, but I had British money in my wallet. However, when I paid, the waiter said the twenty-pound note was an old note (paper) and it was no longer valid. As it happened, I had enough money anyway. I am quite sure the paper note came from the money exchange in Sydney! One would have

thought that they would know such things. I will visit a bank here and see if they will exchange it.

There are many ways of being lost.

I walked right down to the end of Leith Walk, where it veers left to go to the harbour. There are lots of nationalities around. Is this the poorer part of Edinburgh? What was it historically? (I am thinking of family history.)

I note that the Mackie family had to go to Liverpool to board their ship for Australia in 1852. It would have been a long trip, before they even boarded the ship.

Chapter 17: Another search for ancestors

Today's venture is to find the Scottish Genealogical Society at 15 Victoria Place and see what I can find out. It started off a sunny morning and then became cloudy, although it remained warm enough. I got the tram uptown to the Princes Road stop. Google Maps said it wasn't far, just the other side of the park. I walked towards the Castle and then couldn't find it. I found parts of Edinburgh I have not seen before. I think I walked in large spirals.

Finally, I found myself in High Street, which is the real tourist zone. I was outside St Columba's and the ex-church that was advertising the Edinburgh Festival. I was only two minutes away from my destination and I had just walked up a very long flight of stairs, so I sat and had a coffee.

The route to my destination was short but devilish: retrace my steps for twenty metres, turn left, just before the flight of stairs that I had just ascended, and go down a shorter flight of stairs that seems to lead to a small private courtyard.

However, it didn't. Once at the bottom, you turn left and you discover that 15 Victoria Terrace is right there, and the terrace continues into an outside bar. If you keep walking through the bar, you end up in a square and you are back in High Street. Devilish.

There was a door, which was just ajar. I went in. it was clearly a research space, with cabinets and shelves everywhere. There were two older women sitting at computers. One of them, who had two walking sticks, asked me straightaway who I was looking for. No "Hello", no formalities or preliminaries.

I started with Ellen Welch. I had no notes and no laptop, but I remember a lot, so I told her what the problem was. She started work, using Ancestry, then Find My Past, then Family Search. She was very quick, but I could keep up. She had a second monitor set up as a duplicate. It was as large as mine back home, so everything was easy to read. It is so nice when the elementary things have been taken care of.

She checked against numerous family trees in Ancestry, and I told her the ones that were off-track. She honed the essential details, then went back to see what she could find in Fife. She didn't find anything more or less than I had, but it was good validation. It seemed clear that no one in the other family trees had cottoned onto what I had, that she had been in Glasgow with a child, and then straight after, had been on a ship to Australia as a single unmarried female.

She looked at the Migration Form that had been signed off on her arrival in Sydney, and suggested that perhaps she had been working for William Goodsir in Edinburgh, one of her referees. William and his wife had several children, and he was a bootmaker, so Ellen could have been a servant of the household.

The researcher looked for Thomas Welch (the child), but unsuccessfully.

The next topic was Robert Bridges, to see whether we could find his marriage to Margaret Richy in Edinburgh in 1748. She tried in several ways, but it did not surface. Looking at other family trees in Ancestry, she found a couple that said Robert and Margaret had got married in the home parish, St Andrews and St Leonards. But this would contradict the reason for the church council meeting.

Did those people get it wrong? They also had a baptism for one of their children: Catherine (who was born in 1759). I need to look for this. [Later: yes, I have the details.] Otherwise, my whole case collapses. It would have to mean that the parish council meeting was about two different people. I can pursue that at home. [Later: There are no records for the marriage of Robert Bridges and Margaret Richy. I believe I have it correct. And there was no other couple with whom I could have confused them.]

By 1:30 pm, I had had enough. I think my researcher had too, so we quit. I spent twenty-five pounds on membership of the society. It might be useful. I could have donated the money, but she encouraged me to join.

I wandered around lost for a while, going back over my steps in some cases. Two factors: I wasn't clear enough about my next destination so, partly, I was just wandering. And, I was observing myself to see if frustration and irritation were arising. Can I wander lost and still avoid these demons?

I found a pleasant-looking café and went in for some lunch: a grilled cheese sandwich with onion jam, and tea. Yum. A couple of doors up, there was a second-hand bookshop, called the Edinburgh Bookshop. I went in, just to look. It was a tight space, with books stacked high on shelves as well as books shelved normally. The carpet was cut off in places where it had worn out. There were stairs down to a basement. It said that was for music, so I didn't need to go down.

There were lots of books on Scotland, and in the end I did buy one book: *The Silent Traveller in Edinburgh*. At a book fair in Sydney some years ago I had bought *The Silent Traveller in London*, and this book seemed fitting to my current situation. It was the same author, a Chinese man who wrote the books in the 1940s. He was exiled from China and separated from his family. His books were popular in Britain: his name was Chiang Yee. It cost me six pounds.

[Later: I not only discovered *The Silent Traveller in London* in my collection (originally published in 1938; my edition is from 1948), but I also had *The Silent Traveller in Lakeland* (first published 1937; my edition 1949).]

I got lost again trying to find the way to Princes Street, but I found the Kings Stables Road, which goes by a church and graveyard, and yes, I got some photos of the graveyard. It was lovely.

What will I do tomorrow?

Traveling is not something you're good at, it's something you do. Like breathing.

Gayle Forman

Chapter 18: A stroll up to Arthur's Seat

Another Edinburgh day; it threatened rain, but in the end it didn't rain, and although it was occasionally warm, in the end it was a little bit chilly and windy.

My last day in Edinburgh before I head south, and I set out to walk to the top of Arthur's Seat. Along the way I passed Holyrood Palace. Apparently, the Royal family use it from time to time. I didn't see the necessity of inspecting the residence or the grounds.

Arthur's Seat is a hill that slides up to a summit from one side and looks down from there. It is the remnant of a volcano that erupted 325 million years ago. (Mount Warning in New South Wales erupted around 23 million years ago.) Arthur's Seat is named because of some perceived connection to King Arthur of Camelot fame, although nothing specific seems to be known about that. It's 250 metres high, and there is a long rocky track through grassy slopes to the top. Dozens of other people thought it was a good idea to walk up there too. It was steep going, and my lungs and legs had to work hard.

However, I made it to the top. There were a few young children amongst the throng, and some groups of teenage schoolchildren, and one man with a white stick for the sight-impaired. His companion was assisting him. There were lots of nationalities.

Though the traveller may be blind, he knows the road.

Chinese proverb

At the top, you get a magnificent view of Edinburgh and all around. You can see the bridges that cross the Firth of Forth, and the whole southern coastline of Fife. There was cloud, but also big parts bathed in sunshine. It was windy up there.

A helicopter was doing some kind of work in a field below, carrying something across the terrain. It's not often you get the chance to look down on a helicopter that is flying. It reminded me of the time in the McKellar Ranges west of Lismore in about 1976 when I was walking up a ridge and an F-111 fighter jet flew down the valley, hugging the contours with its technology. I looked down on it, and you could see the pilot in the cabin, although only briefly, because a second later there was a loud boom; it had broken the sound barrier.

On the way back down from Arthur's Seat there is a plateau, and I asked two girls if they would photograph me, which they did. They were from New York. Photos of Glenn on location.

Further down the track a lady in front of me slipped on the gravel and fell down. She got a bit of a shock. I helped her up, and she was okay. She went on her way, a bit bruised.

Almost at the bottom, a short American lady asked me if the climb was worth it. I considered what to say. I said, "You won't think so until you get to the top, but then you will."

When I got back down to the bottom, I had to try to find my way back to the city. I saw a graveyard which went up a hill, so I walked through there. Suddenly I had forgotten about being lost or found. It was called the New Calton Graveyard, and I thought it might be near the Old Calton graveyard where I had been the other day. It was; for once I was right.

One of the gravestones I read said it was for Thomas Thompson, who died at age forty-one, having sorted the mail at the post office for over twenty years. That's quite a story. Was the inscription to honour him, or was there nothing else to say about him?

I had some lunch and then got the tram back "home" (it was a five-day pass, and you can ride as many times as you like). I went back to the flat, finished reading a book, then packed it up with some others and went back into town to post another package of books back to home in Sydney. The post office was in a shopping centre near the rail station.

The cost of the postage was thirty pounds. I also managed to change the old twenty-pound note (paper) for two new ten-pound notes (plastic). But in the process, I left my Visa card sitting on the counter. I had just walked out of the shopping centre when the girl who had served me ran up to me with the card. I was grateful!

I wanted to walk to the Writers' Centre again. It was a question of mastering some aspect of navigation, of being able to be found in this landscape. The last time I went there I walked around for an hour, and yet, all the while it had seemed so close. This time I did it fairly promptly and directly. I also figured out why it had been so hard. Google Maps shows you a myriad of options for getting to a destination, and it doesn't remove any of those options once you've started, so that's confusing.

Also, it doesn't tell you how far it is to your destination now. Rather, it continues to show the time for the initial route, so you have no idea about your progress, or whether you have gone off track. The navigator in my car does not work like this. It continually tells you where you are in relation to your target, and if you deviate, it calculates a new route from your current location,

I suppose, or I imagine, that there are options in the app that allow you to control how it works. But there are other difficult factors: my eyesight is not great, and to do that effectively I would need to be sitting down in a room with low light, so the screen would be clear and bright. Then, when I am outside, the screen on the phone is so often drenched with glare that it is a waste of time. What a strange device: it encourages you to live your life in a dark room, like a mushroom!

The other thing is that there are three ways to get into the square (or courtyard) where the centre is. You can come off High Street at two points, which are just narrow openings between shops, or you can come up from the bottom via the Ladies Stairs. I had a cup of tea at the same café as the other day. I didn't go back into the museum. It was enough to have found it without any difficulty.

However, I did discover engravings in the paving stones in the square, that I had not taken notice of before. They were quotes from various famous writers. I took some photos. "This is my own, my native land" (Sir Walter Scott). "We can only pay our debt to the past by putting the future in debt to us" (James Boswell). "Go back far enough and all of humankind are cousins" (Naomi Murtchison). These were some examples.

When I got back to the flat, I tackled the organising of trips and accommodation. I had the route planned: Nottingham to Edinburgh, Edinburgh to St Andrews, accommodation at St Andrews. But it is never simple. Online, the website was extremely slow and unreliable. I entered information, and then it lost it and sent me back to the start. I did eventually get it sorted. I think that people today spend too much time apologising for technology, as if it were a precocious child that still had some minor social flaws. "He didn't really mean to break that lady's vase." "She didn't mean to spill that man's cup of tea." But said child is a prodigious artist (sometimes), so all is forgiven.

Then the bus trip to St Andrews was really difficult. I selected the trip online and went to pay, but at this point it pointed me to my phone, and then it sent me right back to the beginning. It took me ages to sort this out; there were multiple roadblocks in the process. All this with no apologies.

I wanted to get dinner, because I don't know how tomorrow will pan out. I walked up the street and back down the other side. I wanted to get fish and chips. I stopped at the Brunswick Book Club, which was not really a book club; it was a pub. But there were old hardback books strewn around. Mostly they were used to hold cardboard menus that would have blown away in the wind. The one at my table was from 1951 and it was about Scott's expedition to the Antarctic. I have a book in my library at home about this. It was a prize from school.

So, I had a beer (lager, non-alcoholic) and a meal of fish and chips. It was very satisfactory.

I have just started reading *The Silent Traveller in Edinburgh*. Early on he talks about Arthur's Seat. He likens the appearance of it to a reclining elephant. I am favourably disposed to that view of the very large hill.

Chapter 19: A train to Durham

This morning, Wednesday, I leave this abode and board a train for Durham. It's been nice to spend a few days in the same place.

The journey was smooth. I got a tram to St Andrews Square then walked down to the rail station, remembering where the lift was so I didn't have to navigate stairs or escalators with my suitcase. I sat and read for half an hour, then found the right platform for my trip. It was a fast train going to London. I left Edinburgh at 10 am and arrived at Durham at 11:45 am.

The Bridge Hotel was just three minutes' walk from the station, down a curving road, and there was the hotel, right next to a train bridge that had multiple arches. I would guess the hotel is more than a century old. I went in, and there was no one in the bar, but then a lady turned up and said I could go straight into the room, as there was no one in it last night.

It is a pokey hotel room on the first floor with two single beds, and the bathroom is a step down to a lower level. There is a big ledge under the window, which is leadlight and plain glass, and you can put things on the ledge. It has the feel of a small country town with this view. Downstairs is a bar which is frequented mostly by older men. All good.

I made a cup of tea, then got a message on my phone to say my train to Nottingham was leaving now. I checked, and saw that the booking was for today, not Friday. When I booked the ticket, the site kept reverting back to today, and that's what must have happened. I tried to see if I could change the date of the journey, but it was already too late for that.

I rang a phone number from the website, and the lady said I could get a refund, but only if I bought the new ticket to Nottingham. The trouble escalated. I had paid sixty pounds for the ticket, which was much dearer than the ticket from Edinburgh to here. When I looked at the price for the ticket for Friday, it was 120 pounds! I checked alternatives: there were buses, and for trains, different carriers.

However, the options were all awful: one option took fifteen hours and involved multiple changes, et cetera. So I had to take the LNER rail option. I paid the 120 pounds. When I went back to the LNER website to request a refund, you could submit a request, but there was nowhere to provide any explanation, so it doesn't look hopeful, despite the assurances of the lady on the phone. [Later: yes, I did receive the refund without any trouble. It took a few days.]

I was a bit put out by this event. However, I remembered that one of my sons lost the entire price of a flight from Vietnam to Sydney a couple of years ago, because of poor information about visas, and there is nothing I can do about my situation, so I just have to take it. I think, can I be sanguine?

I went out. I was hungry and I needed some food, then I would try to find the famous cathedral. Downtown I found a place to eat, in an upstairs room of a café/bar. The room was saturated with artificial flowers, wall to wall, and the wallpaper itself was covered with flowers. But the meal: haloumi and roasted vegetables on pita bread, was just what I wanted. The man tidying up the dishes asked me how my day was, so I told him my story about the tickets, but I said I was sure I would get over it. I did not want to be seen as the whinging man from Australia.

Walking downtown, it was like a country town that had its grungy side, but after the cafe, one crossed a bridge over the river, and the road rose into a totally different atmosphere. It was old times, and the road was ascending to a square prior to going up to Durham Cathedral. I suspected as much, as I had seen a high spire through the trees from the bridge.

The cathedral was Norman, and it is very rectangular, with square towers at each end. The church is a long rectangle, and the roof is extraordinarily high, and arched. The stained-glass windows are massive. They had a guidebook for sale, but I have one at home which I obtained from my mother. She had visited Durham Cathedral when she came to the UK thirty or forty years ago.

[Later: At home, at first I could not find the booklet. Was I wrong? Then, the next day, I found where I had put it, and there were two copies, from different times. The first copy was published in 1965, and it had stapled inside the back cover a receipt for parking in the "Palace Green" for one shilling. I do not know where this booklet came from; it was not my mother's. The second booklet is definitely my mother's. It was published in 1988 and reprinted in 1990, which corresponds with my mother's visit to England.]

There were many interesting parts of the church, including acknowledgment of women (post-Henry VIII).

I keep thinking of the Eaglestone family as stonemasons, and all the things they might have worked on over the years in Oxford: far more than gravestones or garden walls!

I went to the Durham University library, and there was a tour of a First Folio of Shakespeare's plays, published in 1622. It contained all of his plays, including many that we only know because of the first folios. There are about 200 other First Folios, and there are variations between them.

The notable feature of this folio is that it was stolen (in the 1970s?), and was not recovered for ten years. It was eventually found in America. Apparently, the thief, or a compatriot, had handed it in, at Harvard, I think. He wasn't even an academic or an antique book dealer. He was just some guy whose life was a mess. The book ended up back at Durham. It is currently on display, and there is a facsimile version of it on display as well, which you can touch.

The thief was not kind to the book. He tore the front cover off, and there was some damage to pages. They have decided to leave it as it is. I told the lady about the Japanese concept of Kintsugi, where broken things are patched and mended, but there is no attempt to hide the mending. Gold may be included in the glue. So it is here: the break is accepted as part of the life of the book.

The display was in a library, a large room full of books, with an upper landing as well, with more books. The room looked rather complete, with all the bookshelves seeming to be exactly full. The collection was initially that of the Prince Bishop of the church in the 1600s (this person had temporal as well as religious powers). Eventually the collection came into the possession of the university. I asked how the books were organised. They are ordered into subjects and authors, and above each section there are portraits of those authors, for example, Plato, Erasmus. Could I do anything with this idea for my own library?!

I told the guide that when I was in my twenties, I bought a house in northern Queensland, and inside the house was a glass plaque with the name "Durham House". The name "Durham" stuck in my head since then.

> Wandering re-establishes the original harmony which once existed between man and the universe.
>
> Anatole France

I walked around the streets, and ended up back at the bridge. I remembered that the cathedral was built within a loop of the river, so I thought you might be able to walk around the loop. I started, but then I got distracted, and crossed the river at another bridge, and walked back up to the cathedral that way. That was good, because I hadn't seen this side of the cathedral.

There were residences and clubs along the road. This is the kind of place that has clubs. Note, on the river, there was a sculling club, and people were rowing on the river.

There were some very old trees in a courtyard.

I walked back down to the township and back to the hotel. Do I want dinner? Not seriously, but I won't have breakfast, and I might be hungry by mid-morning. But I don't want to eat in the grungy part of town, and I don't want to spend lots at a tourist restaurant.

The problem was solved when I walked downstairs from my room. You have to go through the bar to exit, and there were just the two girls looking after the bar. They asked me if I wanted a drink, so I sat and had a beer (non-alcoholic) in the bar. Then one of them asked me if I wanted dinner, and she brought out a menu. I hadn't thought food was a possibility here, as the bar was deserted.

I looked through the menu, which was a pub menu, most of which was irrelevant to my diet. However, I supposed that chicken with salad could be tolerable, so I ordered that. When it came it was enormous, as one might expect for a pub, but I got through most of it, and it was quite fine.

The British news was on the television, and it was just like the news at home: rather awful, and orchestrated as a type of entertainment. This was followed by a British sitcom. I got the impression that this was patterned on something like "Neighbours" in Australia. Of course, the pattern is probably in reverse, from Britain to Australia and back again. I display my ignorance (thankfully).

I left the pub. It was still light, so I went for a walk. I turned left then went straight ahead, and walked up the hill. The places on the left were up steep stairways, but I got the impression that the inhabitants had access from the back or the top, as some of the stairways were completely overgrown. The right-hand side of the road was even steeper, and mostly forested.

Near the top of the hill on the right was an entrance, and it was to a church and a cemetery. Even when I am not looking for cemeteries, I find them. The church was St Cuthbert's (Church of England). The cemetery was about an acre. It had been mown recently, just roughly, by a ride-on lawnmower, I assume. The graves were not in good condition; they leaned in all directions. The oldest ones that I could make out were from the 1800s.

I didn't expect to see any familiar names, and I didn't. There are no members of the family tree from this part of the world. One gravestone showed the occupation of the deceased: he was a painter. It is unclear to me whether he was a trade painter or an artistic painter, or whether he was a painter of the sights of Durham. The church was stone, and old, but not so old. It had a square tower but apparently no bells.

It was getting dark, so shadows were falling across the cemetery. I saw a few rabbits running across the grass. I suppose they are not bothered much here.

I walked out of the churchyard and down the road on the other side. It was a four-lane road going down to the town centre. On my right was Wharton Park, up on the hillside. It is mostly forest. There were a couple of people walking through it. I could look right inside the forest, between the leaves.

I wasn't far from the station, from where I had come this morning. I walked along a path leading to the station. There were cars waiting for the next train to arrive, obviously to pick a person up. I found a subway so I could go underneath the railway line, and I found the road that I knew went down to the hotel. But this time I saw other sights that I didn't see this morning: the spires of the cathedral, and other tracks going up the hill and into the city.

It's 9:00 pm and still light. But the light in my room is very faint. It will be no good at all for reading. That's the way of it these days.

The railway track is just above the hotel, so I hear the trains when they pass over.

I have the whole day in Durham tomorrow. Durham University has an Oriental Museum, and I will look at that.

There is a Waterstones bookshop in Durham. I went in it today. It is in the part of town that is equally tourist and also associated with the university. I looked for a while, but there were zero books on the I Ching or even the Tao Te Ching. The quest is languishing.

I bought no books. I was not even tempted.

Chapter 20: The Oriental Museum at Durham

I am thinking of going to the Botanical Gardens as well as the Oriental Museum. It is a fine day. It's supposed to be a thirty-minute walk to the Oriental Museum, but I think Google Maps does not take account of hills, or having to wait for traffic lights, which take the longest time in Durham. It took me the best part of an hour to get there. But I did not make any wrong turns! I begin to think that finding my way around is possible.

It was a long walk uphill, although not too steep. The university occupies most of the surroundings along the road. There are colleges, student rental apartments, and departments of the university.

Near one intersection, there was a gathering of some students, about twenty or so, and they were protesting, holding up signs. As I passed a student, he said, 'What do you think of the staffing cuts?' I replied, 'It's modern life. It's not education; it's business.' I hope I did not disillusion him too much. There were many stories I could have told him, about the subsidence of education in universities into a façade for a form of business.

The Oriental Museum is in a modern building. I arrived just before opening time, 10 am. A carload of old ladies arrived at the same time. They had come to do volunteer work at the museum. On the fringes, there persists respect for scholastic endeavours.

There were four levels to the museum. Ground floor was the top floor. The major theme was the Silk Road, about which I do not know a lot, but obviously it was important for 2,000 or more years, for trade in silk and other goods, and for traffic in ideas. The countries that were featured were Korea, Japan, Indonesia, India, the Afghans, and China. There was also a section on ancient Egypt.

The Korean section looked at scholars, and how they were valued in the culture over a long period. It reminded me of the Netflix series, "The Rookie Historian". The book, *The Silent Traveller in Edinburgh*, remarked on the high status of scholars in China, in contrast to the merchant class, whose sole goal was to make money, whatever it took to do so. They were considered to be a lower class of people.

I liked the exhibitions. There was a wide variety of topics dealt with, and they showed the interaction of Asian people and Europeans. In the China section on the lowest level, I found some reproductions of ancient oracle bones used in divination (the forerunner of the I Ching), and there was a statue of Lao Tzu, the author of the *Tao Te Ching*, seated on a buffalo, about half a metre long.

In the shop I found a bowl of I Ching coins for sale. There really wasn't much in the museum to suggest why the coins were there, aside from the oracle bones. I purchased a few. The lady on the counter asked me about myself, and what work I had done. I told her I had got to my age without having a career, which I considered an achievement. She thought that perhaps that was a little too self-deprecating. I talked a bit about my writing, and about my endeavours in family history. I mentioned Siegfried's story: the German sailor who was also a baron, who married one of my father's cousins in 1939 in Sydney.

She liked the idea that I had written books, and she said she was going to look me up online. She also asked me if I was a Buddhist, or if I meditated, because I seemed to have a presence of peace about me. I said I used the I Ching, but I could not be identified as the member of any group.

Man follows the earth. Earth follows heaven. Heaven follows the Tao. Tao follows what is natural.

Tao Te Ching, Ch. 25

After the museum, I thought I should visit the Botanical Garden. The sign said it was just across the road. But I followed the road, and it went on and on, past student colleges. At one point there was a walking track that went off into the forest, so I followed that. It was a wide trail, and it looked well used, by people wanting time to think. The forest was lovely, and it went down into the valley. At one point there were some squirrels running up into a tree.

The light was lovely on this clear day, sun coming down through the summer leaves. After a while I returned to the road. The Botanical Garden was a bit further back and on the other side of the road. There were quite a few cars parked. I guess most people drive to get here.

I walked down through the gardens for a while. There were many specimen trees from other countries, for example, fir trees and red oaks from north-western America. I had some lunch then walked back.

When I got back to the main square where people start the walk up to Durham Cathedral, I decided to walk back to the hotel a different way. It was a brave decision, a test of my sense of orientation.

Once again, I realised that Google Maps and I do not get on, and I cannot figure out whether I should be going left or right. I walked up through numerous housing estates; mostly small two-storey houses on their own little plots, so quintessentially English to me. Quite a few seemed to be empty. I guess not everyone wants to live in Durham, or rather, they need to live in a bigger city.

I tried several times with Google Maps, but not with much success. I ended up walking right back to near the smaller church in the main square, and then retraced my steps from this morning, and got to my hotel after two hours of misguided walking. I am not sure how to get better at this. It is a burden.

In the town, in one of many side streets, I found The People's Bookshop. It contained a mixture of old radicalism and new gender alliances. I had a slow look. The interesting find was a whole section on mining in Durham. They used to mine for coal. Maggie Thatcher put a stop to that, with a long strike that aimed to break the mining unions. The bitterness about that still seems fresh here, and it is reflected in the books and in the people.

I had a look through the selection on mining, but I did not buy anything. It was a bit remote from Cornish mining, where the object was tin and copper. [Later: I wondered, is there coal in Cornwall? Answer: No, there is no coal in Cornwall. While Cornwall is known for its rich mining history, particularly for tin and copper, the coal deposits found in other parts of the British Isles and Ireland, like South Wales, are not present in Cornwall. Historically, coal was imported from South Wales to power the mines and other industries in Cornwall.]

I had a coffee in a small shop in an alley. Two girls beside me were talking about boys. There seemed to be a belief that all problems needed to be put into words, and once you had put them into words, all problems would be solved. I don't think these premises are exactly false, but I think they are faulty. What it seems to lead to is that young people spend a lot of time talking about their feelings. Moreover, their feelings are treated as sacrosanct and central. At the extreme, this means that self-pity is defensible.

On the outside wall of the town library was a quote in large letters: "Only you can write the next page." (Of course, it was in ALL CAPS.)

Have I seen enough of Durham? Yes, for now. There is that tension between the old and the new. The church created so much, but its power is no longer felt. And there is always the question of whether things are always only about the nature of the ruling class. We still have a ruling class; it's just a bit different to what it was then.

And we are stuck. Like the cemetery I saw last night, we have all those graves that we think we should honour and respect, but no one knows who the people were, and for the most part, they probably never will. The "sensible" thing would be to pull them all out, and perhaps put them in the corner of a park somewhere, as I did see in one place today.

We have created so much, but we no longer understand it. So much we think is irrelevant now, and we are weighed down by it. When the Korean scholars, or the Scottish novelists, wrote an essay or a novel, they bound it and kept it, as if the writings were of permanent value. What now? I have been in many bookshops on my trip, and I could never read all those books, and if I did, what would I come away with?

People like to make statements like the one on the outside library wall: "Only you can write the next page." People have said to me, about particular topics we had been discussing, "You should write a book about that", but would they read it? The irony is that in some cases, I had already written a book about the topic we were discussing.

It's funny. The lady at the museum today, said that about the story of Siegfried, which I had recounted to her in one paragraph: "You should write a book about that!" Well, I did. The book is "out there".

I never heard back from the museum at Holzminden, in Germany. I wrote to them three months ago to ask them if they had any information on Baron Von Einseidel, the man who was also a sailor called Siegfried Hottelmann. Holzminden is where his ancestral lands were. Is it possible that no one at the museum spoke English?

Only some things are possible. As well, it seems that only some things may be known.

What the I Ching says is that our attitude is central. This protects us against self-pity. What would I do if I rejected self-pity, or refused to countenance it? Then the tree would rise up out of the ground (46, Sheng). It would occupy the space that was implied in its seed.

I went out for dinner. I have many constraints on choice. Not too expensive, a cooking style that is likely to give me vegetarian options, and rice would be good. And don't spend too much time dismissing options and running out of choices. Accordingly, I chose a place that had sushi and some other things. I opted for fried tofu and rice. It was cheap, and basic, but that's all that was needed. It was more take-away than a sit-down restaurant, but there were a few chairs.

While I was eating, a young couple came in to get some food to take away. They were loaded down, especially the man. He had a giant backpack, one of those that could contain a tent, sleeping bags and a week's supply of food as well as implements for cooking. She had a backpack, more modest in size but still heavy, and a carry bag. The carry bag had a teddy bear on top, similar to the bear I had when I was young, Edward Bear.

Somehow, bears always manage to look dignified, no matter what the circumstances. He was observing the scene he was in. So, I don't know what their story was, but it looked like it involved camping out, and they were both content with what they were doing. They bought some food and took it away with them. The bear was also a traveller, observing, pondering.

I walked home, managing to not get lost on the way. A positive achievement, although the challenge level was not high. On the way, two young men with Irish accents asked me if I knew the way to the station. After today, you might think I would be the last person to ask. However, this afternoon, at the same intersection, I overheard a conversation between two people: a man was taking a woman to the station. They had been involved in a seminar at Durham University, and he was the local, so he was showing her the way and explaining it to her as well.

So now, I was able to say, "Yes, you take those stairs there, and that will take you straight up to the station." But I couldn't help adding, "That's one question I do know the answer to." And I wish to add, that to my credit, the station was not visible from where we were standing.

Chapter 21: Train journey to Nottingham

Today is a day of travel. I go from Durham to Nottingham. I have scoped out the steps. I have to make two changes of train: one at York and the next at Newark. But at Newark, there are two separate rail stations, and they are a mile apart. I suppose there are historical reasons for this, inconvenient though it is. I think I will have to get a taxi. There is about thirty minutes between one arrival and the next departure.

And I have to vacate the Bridge Hotel by 10 am, but my train doesn't come until 1 pm. I don't want to lug a suitcase around for three hours. I could find somewhere and sit and read. I am working my way through *The Silent Traveller in Edinburgh*. The book mentions many places I have been to, and he talks about "closes", which seem to be a specifically Edinburgh feature.

I am going to visit my nephew and his family, and have spread out all the gifts I brought, to consider to whom I should give them.

I have been in the UK now for over three weeks. Time passes. It has been interesting, and I have seen many things. It will be good to get home and sit and think about all the things. Perhaps I am a scholar in the traditional Korean sense of the word. It is expected that scholars will think about things and write about them. It is not assumed that they will publish them, and the writings are not merely a record of events; they are a record of thinking.

The day's travel was long. I checked out of the hotel at 10 am, and I just walked up to the station and waited there. I read my book. At least there was a place there to buy coffee and something to eat. It was another warm day in England, a bit much for most people, comfortable for me. The view from the platforms at Durham is of dense forest all along the other side of the platform. It is lovely that this is the case in what is, after all, a city.

The train came. It was crowded. Trains go from here to London, Plymouth and other places in the south. There is no provision for baggage, and I had to hug my suitcase between my knees. For this I paid 120 pounds. The trip was only about forty minutes. The train was late. There is a non-stop volley of announcements saying they are sorry, but you still have to deal with the consequences. (The cynical would say that the announcements are just a cost of doing business.)

It meant that when I arrived at York, I only had a couple of minutes to get to the next platform, wherever that was. When they send you the ticket information, they don't tell you what the final destination of the train is, so you look at the boards and you have no idea which train you are meant to be catching. And there were about a dozen platforms at York. I went down in an escalator, which got me to a subway, then I had to go up onto another platform and find somebody to ask. It was a new way of being lost.

Once I found out, I had to go through the ritual again, of going down in the lift and getting to the right platform. When I did get to the right platform, I discovered that the train was already there. I was in carriage G. I thought I would have to get on the first carriage and then walk through, assuming the carriages were numbered A to G. And this would be difficult with my luggage.

I got up into the third carriage and discovered it was carriage G! Again I had to hug my suitcase in front of me. There was a man sitting next to me who was going to Leeds to attend the wedding of a relative. He was in his sixties, and obviously a hard worker. He said he worked on transmission lines all over the country. He had a broad accent (which I couldn't name), and sometimes I couldn't pick up what he was saying.

We chatted. He was at a stage behind me with the technology. He had got his ticket on this phone, but he didn't know how to show the ticket to the conductor. I think the conductor wasn't interested, so he told the man to download the app and open it, and he would come back. So, the man managed to do that, but I don't know if it finished downloading, and I wasn't much help. I saw the conductor a couple of times down the corridor, but he obviously wasn't interested in coming back.

The next station was Newark Northgate. I knew that the station I had to get to was Newark Castle. It seems to be a twenty or thirty-minute walk between the two stations. I spoke to a young attendant. I saw lots of cars parked outside in the carpark, but there was no sign of a bus or a taxi. The attendant was very didactic about it. He said, "Have you got your phone? Go to Google Maps. Type in Newark Castle, then get it to tell you what way to go. It will take you twenty minutes." And that was where he decisively cut off communication with me. He had obviously been through the worst versions of this scenario and faced angry passengers.

I left Google Maps on voice, and it was admittedly good. It took me on laneways and footbridges, all the way without mishaps, except it wasn't sure exactly where I needed to be at the station: this platform or the other, which was across a level crossing at the far end of the station.

There was a drama about the next train. The board said it was cancelled, then another board asserted that it was delayed. I heard people saying there was something on the tracks towards Leicester, which was the train's destination. Then a young boy who looked about sixteen came along, but he was in uniform, and he said (with all the authority of a uniform) that the train would be going to Nottingham, but they weren't sure after that. I flashed back to the jigsaw on the footpath in London with the pieces scattered around randomly.

And the train did come. This was a different railway line from the earlier train; it was East Midlands. The train was crowded; again, there was nowhere for baggage. But in the area near the doors, there were a couple of little folding seats that popped down from the wall, so I sat on one of them and nursed my luggage. For 120 pounds.

A good walker leaves no tracks.

Tao Te Ching, Ch. 27

I got to Nottingham, another large railway station, and I found my nephew, or rather, he found me. We went to a nearby hotel and had a drink. It was called The Vat and Fiddle. The building next door is the tax office. The name of the pub was felt by the locals to be ironic.

We walked across town and then we caught a bus to their neighbourhood. It was a double decker bus and we went upstairs, only because my nephew was now carrying my bags. We got to some neighbourhood shops after ten to fifteen minutes and alighted. We bought hot food for dinner, then walked down the hill to his place.

I have a room downstairs, which is cool and roomy. This whole area used to have coal mines, so there is concern about subsidence. It reminded me about coal around Durham as well. And I realised I had never heard Cornish people talking about coal mining. But I had worked out the answer to that question at Durham: there is no coal in Cornwall.

I met my two grand nieces. Apparently, they were looking forward to my visit. The older one is having her first communion tomorrow at the local Catholic Church. Her mother is Irish, and she is Catholic. I had bought an appropriate card for a first communion, before I left Sydney, and a small gift.

The budding communicant dressed up in her ornate long white dress with layers of frills, and pretty shoes. There was also a veil that had some history to it. She was delighted. In contrast, her younger sister chose to wear to the church ceremony her football jersey that had her name embroidered on the back of it, and a large number four. It seemed like a statement of confident individuality.

The ceremony was around ninety minutes long. There was a lot of singing by the children, supported by a local schoolchildren's choir. The accompanying instrument was not an organ, but an amplified guitar, which was perfect for the occasion. I found the children's singing very moving. The priest said lots of prayers. There were readings from the Bible. Interestingly, the coordination of the event was done by a woman, not a man or a priest.

The church is modern, so the architecture is a modern design. There was lots of stained glass, which was not traditional, but an abstract pattern. I didn't mind it.

There is a whole history about Catholics in the community in England. It occurs mostly in the northern parts of England, not nearly so much in the south. It has to do with patterns of migration, and historical patterns of seasonal migration for work, mostly of Irish people.

The children had their first communion, and then all the Catholic people in the congregation had communion. The priest said he hoped that "some of" the children would feel the presence of the Lord and the significance of the occasion.

The older girl seemed pleased that she had carried it off, and had been part of the throng. She belongs, along with all the other children, in this great entity. As people left the church, there was all that milling that occurs. Two ladies were sitting at a table at the back selling little Catholic artefacts that children might like: cards, rosaries and the like. It didn't seem that too many families felt the necessity for that.

We got back home, and the older girl divested herself of her adornments and put on shorts and tee-shirt. She was attempting to perfect standing on her hands. A variety of people began turning up, with food and children, so the backyard turned into a festival of games, trampoline, swings and a blow-up pond, taking advantage of the warm weather.

There were many conversations taking place in different rooms and outside: the lounge room, the kitchen, and out on the deck. I had many conversations during the afternoon too. I was Australian, so there is always something to be said about that, and I have many family history stores to tell. And I have my current travels for comment.

There was some discussion of how we can live in the moment when we also have to consider the past and plan for the future. There was talk about why people see themselves as being English, or Australian, or Irish. One man said he was Scottish. He was born in Scotland and he spent the first nine years of his life there, despite the fact that both of his parents are Irish, and despite the fact that most of his classmates were Presbyterian and he was Catholic.

My nephew's wife was an Irish woman in England. My nephew was English, but his mother was from Australia. I don't usually identify as an Australian, not if that means I have to know about, and love, cricket and football or surf lifesaving, but Australia is in my bones. Do I get lost in Australia? Perhaps I do, but that is not the impression that remains. In a new place, I find my way; I expect to be able to. The sun comes up in the east and floats up into a clear sky. The shadows track the day.

The next day my niece visited us with one of her two children. We went down to the river, the River Trent. Along the banks of the river are big steps, probably for people to sit and watch boating events, or rowing events. While we were sitting there eating lunch, a tourist boat came past us: *The Princess*. The people waved to us. So there I was, the solitary traveller waving to the tourists.

The rain had been threatening, but after a few drops, it decided to forbear. It was overcast but kind. It was a day off for me, a whole day without being lost, because someone else was holding the reins.

Chapter 22: A long day on buses

I am leaving Nottingham. My nephew drove me to the bus station. Again, I found it difficult to locate myself, especially in trying to rely on technology. I was at a bus station with sixteen bays. Which was the correct bay? I was going all the way to Edinburgh, where I would change (I knew the bus station there) and catch a bus to St Andrews, over on the east coast of Fife.

There was a touch-screen, but I couldn't get it to respond to my typing, so I left it alone before I could get upset about it and wonder why this was happening. I went for the human alternative: I asked two men in yellow uniforms. This doesn't always work, because sometimes the people in uniforms might just be security guys who are not responsible for whether passengers are lost, only if they become violent or threatening to other passengers. They don't necessarily know anything about buses.

But they did know, and they told me to walk around to the other side of the building, to Bay One, and I would find the bus I wanted. Which I did. The question about the technology had slunk into the corner of my mind, still a sullen presence, but I dispelled it. One likes things to work, and to fulfil their intended function. But I was not responsible for the technology, and fortunately, the humans were helpful. This what one relies on.

The bus had come from Leicester (twenty-seven miles south) and it was going through to Glasgow after Edinburgh. It was crowded, but during the day, more people got off than got on. A lot of people went to Leeds. When we got to Leeds, the driver casually announced that he needed a break, so the bus would be there for twenty minutes. It was an odd announcement. He said that if anybody wanted a smoke, now was the time to do it. It was unclear to me, was this an interruption to the schedule, or part of it?

You couldn't see much from inside the bus. I was in a section where the window had pixels all over the glass, so the view was obscured. I'm sure it was a terrific picture on the outside. And it was difficult to see the landscape around the tall seats and the people sitting. I saw tiny snippets of scenery, occasionally. At one point we went past where Lindisfarne is, and the Holy Island: the first Christians in England, before 1000 AD. We were going along the east coast of England.

We stopped at Newcastle briefly. Horace Waller, the bigamist in my family history, had come from Newcastle-on-Tyne. Horace had married my father's first wife; after two months she discovered that he was already married, not once but twice, and was not divorced from either of them. My father came along after this and married her. After a few years, she died of heart troubles. But I didn't think I would learn much by spending time in Newcastle.

As we drove into Edinburgh, we went past Topping & Co. Bookshop. I had been there already; I had explored whether they had any I Ching books. I had bought a small book about the philosophy of the home (at the moment, defined as a place where one is never lost).

I had had something small to eat at Leeds, and a drink, but I didn't have anything more until we got to Edinburgh, about 5:30 pm. I was hungry and dehydrated, and I felt bad. There was a machine to get drinks at the Edinburgh Bus Station, but my head wouldn't work properly, and I couldn't figure it out. Fortunately, there was a small café at one end of the bus station, and I could get a sandwich and drink there: by talking to humans, not by trying to figure out buttons on a machine. I started to feel a bit better.

The bus to St Andrews left about seven pm. I found my ticket, but the driver said he couldn't get it to work. Apparently, you are supposed to "activate" it just before you get on the bus. I had activated it in the morning because I thought I should have it ready. But the driver, after giving me a lecture about it in a broad Scottish accent which I could just manage to decipher, left it at that. I guess he has to deal with it a lot.

He wasn't being angry with me; he was talking out of his frustration. Technology is a strange and arbitrary country. How is a person supposed to know such a bizarre thing? I was simply trying to be prepared, so I didn't have a crisis of dysfunction while I was standing in a queue.

It helps if you consider that this is the Stone Age of the Internet. Things will often be a little rough, illogical, or mystifyingly dysfunctional.

The road from Edinburgh to St Andrews was quite decent. I was expecting a narrow country road, as in the country west of Cork, but much of the way it was highway. It was still light: the long afternoon and extended sunset. He stopped at a few places, like Falkland. There were places where there were largish shopping centres. Soon after we left Edinburgh, we drove across a high bridge over the Firth of Forth. I could see the two other bridges as well: the railway bridge, and the new road bridge with two high pillars and cables, rather like the Anzac Bridge in Sydney.

We got to the bus station at St Andrews around nine pm. I turned on the voice on Google Maps to find my way, because this had worked for me the other day. I set it to Agnes Blackadder, the student accommodation at the university. It was quite clear: turn right, go the roundabout and turn left. I walked for thirty minutes, but the directions were becoming unclear, not corresponding to the streets. I was so angry. I was tired. It had been a long day, and it was gradually getting dark. And the sign-in time was notionally before ten o'clock.

Eventually I walked all the way back to the bus station, all the way back to the start. I checked the phone again, but I had to decide, against what it appeared to be saying, to go left instead of right from the bus station. The app still wasn't clear to me. The distance was supposed to be about ten minutes. I had spent more than half an hour walking, and I was back to my starting point. This time, after I started, there was a road leading in a direction that seemed to fit with the phone.

> The superior person knows that to achieve an enduring end, they must be aware of their mistakes at the beginning.
>
> I Ching, 54, John Blofeld

With a bit of patience, I managed to find myself outside the correct student accommodation building in the grounds of the university. Fortunately, there were two American men who had just arrived in their car, and they had just got access to inside the building, and they let me in. In a minute, the warden came, and he gave us our keys. I found my room on the second floor. There are hundreds of rooms and several floors of the building, so there was a lift. There was still the danger that I would lose myself in the corridors, but I managed to find my way in a straightforward manner.

Could I credit increasing competency for this small success, and would it persist tomorrow? It was hard to say, because it seemed that I found my way by going against what the app appeared to be saying.

The room is a student room, adequate but tiny, with very little floor space. But there is a kettle, so I can make a cup of tea. I read from my book for a little while, then slept.

Chapter 23: St Andrews and Kilconquhar

This was the first place I had been in where they actually had a breakfast as part of the deal (except for Durham Bridge Hotel, where we got a plate with a granny smith apple, a chocolate muffin and a yoghurt bar; I ate the apple). I expected this to be a thwarted provision as well, because I usually only have fruit salad and yoghurt for breakfast, and occasionally a piece of toast. But they serve dozens of people here, and during term, probably hundreds, so there was a comprehensive kitchen and many staff. They had servings of fruit salad: from cans, not fresh, but it is something, and yoghurt.

And I had a piece of toast. The toaster had a rolling conveyor belt, and the bread moved along and got cooked along the way. It came out at the bottom. I had seen this before, in Hobart at the 100-year-old Astor Private Hotel. A German girl wanted to cook toast, and she looked puzzled, but I think she had watched someone before, so she got the idea.

There were lots of children, either with their parents or in groups. I think it is school holidays, and there are workshops happening at the university.

Check-out is in two days' time, so I have to decide this morning where I am going next.

It was quite cool today, although it didn't rain. I wandered (such is my bravery). I went up through the town. Waterstones Bookshop is here, so I went in. I am fairly sure they had no I Ching books, but my head was still shaky after yesterday's experience, and my eyes couldn't focus properly, Unpleasant. By the afternoon, my eyes had settled down and I could read comfortably.

I walked into a square which was now part of a college of the university. There was a tour group nearby. I think the square had a gruesome history in the 1500s: the burning to death of a man who was deemed to be a heretic. This story seemed to be replicated elsewhere in town. The square was called Hebdomadar's Block.

I walked towards the sea and there is a museum there which is an old castle from when Christianity arrived in Scotland in about 800 AD. Supposedly the bones of St Andrew, one of the disciples of Jesus, were brought here. Many pilgrims came to St Andrews over the next few hundred years, through to the Middle Ages. The Benedictine monks were here. Of course, there was trouble once the Reformation started, and schisms.

There is a museum with parts of the story, and parts of the castle are still standing, and you can walk up on it. There was a group of Americans there when I was there. You can still see fireplaces, and alcoves, and viewing places, where guards watched for threats from over the sea. I enjoyed my visit. I wonder how my family fitted into that history, or whether they were practical people who lived their lives and left the church to itself.

Down the street there was an obelisk which was a monument to martyrs: It was built in the 1840s. I took a photo. Martyrs? What was that about? There were four martyrs in all, around the same time, who spoke against Catholicism. The first was Patrick Hamilton in

1528. He had been to Europe and had been influenced by Martin Luther. But there were three other martyrs commemorated too.

There was a large area dedicated to golf, and of course, there were many people (mainly men) out playing. My impression was of lots of green. There were plenty of shops selling golfing gear and clothes. I cannot confess to any interest in golf.

I went into an Oxfam shop to look at their books. They had quite a few on Scotland, but I bought none. My needs are quite narrow.

I ate some late lunch at a student union café: cheap and adequate.

There are many small streets like the closes in Edinburgh. Some are called closes here too.

I went to the Natural History Museum, which had artefacts from geological times, when Scotland was a volcanic region, and situated close to the Equator. There were stone and bronze tools and weapons from 8,000 BC from the Picts and later people: Vikings. The Romans didn't make it to Scotland in a dominant way. They may have had a camp here and there in Fife. There was a Scottish scientist in the mid-1850s who found many fossils and who was renowned.

There were Polish soldiers in Scotland during World War 2. I learned that too.

There was an exhibit about schooling in the 1830s in Scotland and later. I spoke to a lady at the museum about my quest, and she said that perhaps I would be able to find some school records of my family.

I have extended my stay here at the students' quarters for four more nights. I will get back to Edinburgh to be able to go to the Sarah Blasko concert. Today, I will go to Cupar.

No, a change of plans: the people at the family history society at Cupar are only there on Friday and Saturday. So, I am going to see Kilconquhar today (Wednesday). Google Maps suggests that you need two buses: one towards Edinburgh, and then one back this way again. When I got to the bus station, there were several different opinions among people I spoke to: one was to go towards Edinburgh, but it wasn't clear about the second bus; one bus towards Dundee, which didn't sound right, even to me. Time passed, and I thought I would have to abandon it. Lost again?

The timetables at the bus station didn't help much. Google Maps seemed to favour going to Edinburgh and coming back. Then, a bus arrived, X95, and it was going to Leven via the village of Kilconquhar. I could come back the same way. The cost was 2.20 pounds. (Mysteriously, the journey back cost me 6.60 pounds. I am not even going to think about that.)

He who loses the way feels lost. When you are at one with the Tao, the Tao welcomes you.

Tao Te Ching, Ch. 23

It was a double-decker bus, on the narrow roads. I am glad I am not driving. The bus went down the coast from St Andrews, and around the coast until he got to the village of Kilconquhar, which is a little bit inland. He did a couple of loops along the way to go into retirement villages and the like. There was a flow of people in and out, young and old, babies, prams, small children, dogs, walking sticks.

We stopped at many towns, including Kingsbarn, Crail, Anstruther, Pittenween, Elie, Earlsferry, St Monance. Pittenweeem was a fishing village; it looked like the only one that was currently a fishing port. All the other places were agricultural: pasture, cattle, sheep. crops, hot-houses. Most of these towns had turned up in my family history research. Alexander Mackie and Rachel Bridges had emigrated to Australia in 1852 with all of their children. Alexander was born in

Earlsferry; Rachel was born in St Monance. The parents of both of them came from the same parts, all born within a few miles of each other.

Most of the buildings in all of the villages were old stone houses, say 100-300 years old. But everyone is living a version of the modern life. I'm sure they all shop and vote.

I think about members of my family leaving here and not coming back. What does Australia think Scotland is like? What do the Scottish think we are like, in Australia? For me, it is more precise than that, especially now, sitting on a bus and being driven through these towns. My ancestors came from these particular places. The entity Scotland is somewhat more abstract. But I remember a song by the Australian singer, Jodi Martin (no relation), who said, "I knew I was Australian, on the other side of the world". I guess the Scots knew that they were Scots once they arrived in Australia.

What part does Kilconquhar play in my family history? It relates to a story told to me by my mother when I was a child. It was a romance, which I have told in two of my earlier books (*All the Rivers Come Together*, and *Ordinary People, Remarkable Lives*). I think that Robert Bridges (born 1719, died 1791) worked at Kilconquhar House when he was young. Maybe he worked as a groom; there were always horses that needed attending to. But he left and went to Edinburgh, where he obtained work at Edinburgh Castle and learned how to be a baker. He also met a girl there, Margaret Richy, and they got married and moved back to Fife.

That is one story about Kilconquhar House. There is also another. I think that Alexander Mackie and Rachel Bridges may have worked there in the 1820s, when they were young. They were the ones who emigrated to Australia in 1852. Alexander later became a weaver, and then a stonemason, but it is not hard to imagine that he worked at the great house as a groom, and Rachel worked there as a maid.

Kilconquhar House was originally Kilconquhar Castle, owned by the Earls of Fife going back to the 1200s. It was rebuilt as a baronial mansion house in the 1500s, and was purchased in 1764 by the Lindsay family. The current owner is the sixteenth Earl of Lindsay. An engraving of the house was published in the *Scots Magazine and Edinburgh Literary Miscellany* in 1812. Unfortunately, a fire destroyed much of the house in the 1970s and it has been rebuilt. It still has accommodation on the grounds, a restaurant in the house itself, and equestrian activities.

The bus driver let me off in the middle of the village of Kilconquhar around midday: sunny, silent, and also no place to eat or even have a drink of water. It was a long day in that respect, but I knew I could do it. The village is a tidy place, with mostly up-market cars.

I didn't head straight out to the estate. I decided to tackle the graveyard at the church first. It was a stone church with a square tower. It had one bell that chimed the hours. There was no minister around; I was alone in the graveyard. A large section of it was modern, that is, post-1900. It is an active cemetery. Among the old graves, there are about half that have fallen over, and a quarter that are unreadable.

I looked slowly and thoroughly for surnames that rang a bell. "Ritchie" might be a connection (I have Richy in the family tree), and there were a couple of others. There were some impressive graves and tombs that were for the rich or the prominent, or the military.

I looked quickly through the modern part of the cemetery, but all the names were unfamiliar. I think spending more time here would be no more rewarding. Yet, it is very quiet in the cemetery, especially on a sunny day. Few people in the town stirred. One man was trimming his garden, the occasional vehicle crept from one end of town to the other, two men were doing home renovations or maintenance.

I walked out towards the estate. It is signposted, and there is a golf course there. It was a kilometre (or shall we say, half a mile?) from the centre of town. There was a stone gateway off to the right. I walked all the way up and over the hill. Then I saw some cabins (maybe a dozen), separate to each other, with their own carparks. To the left was what could have been a practice golf-driving range.

I walked down past the cabins until I came to the grand house, just as described on its website. It now houses Lindsay's Restaurant, and has done so for the last twenty-one years. I think that any accommodation must be in the outlying cabins, unless it is somewhere behind the great house.

There were three people horse riding in the near-distance: clip-clop, and exchanging small-talk. Nearby was a stone pond, with flowers and ornaments. Along a pathway walked a mature, well-dressed lady. She spoke to me (with American accent), to ask if I wanted anything. I said I was visiting from Australia, and my three-times great grandparents had left Scotland in 1852 for Australia, but before that I think they had worked here, as servants in the house.

The lady was quite warmed by my story. She said, "It is lovely to go back and find your roots", and she wished me well. Her husband picked her up in the car. They had been staying here.

The big house was shut up. The restaurant must open at nighttime. I thought there was no use banging on the door. I think I came here to tell stories, as much as my intention was to further my knowledge and add to the stories. I have taken many photos. I have the feeling of the past, and the trials my ancestors put themselves to in search of a new start. So that's what I have to see it as: a new start.

I walked back to town, still hungry and thirsty, but satisfied. There was a hotel (inn?) down near the gate to the church, but I had read the sign: it opens some evenings, from 5 pm to 7 pm. It looked dark and shut up when I walked past it.

I waited for twenty minutes at the bus stop, and a bus came, going back to St Andrews. It was again an engaging trip. On the way, you can see the island out in the Firth of Forth. I think it's called the Isle of May. There are ferry trips out to it, but it doesn't look very hospitable.

At St Andrews, I got off near town, and walked straight up to a shop to have a sandwich and a juice. After that, I walked back to the dormitory to put my pack down. I took my laptop today, because I wasn't sure if I'd need it. It was heavy, but I did write down some families I was looking for: Alexander Mackie and Elizabeth Simpson's parents, so I knew what to be on the lookout for.

In town, I went to the Tourist Information Centre. I wanted to ask them about travelling to Cupar and Markinch. The girl had time, so I told her some stories. I told her about today, and she loved the story of Alexander and Rachel working at the great house. I told her the story of tomorrow: Ellen and her father, the coal-mining manager, how she got pregnant, ran away, had to give away the child (Thomas), went to Australia and married a convict, and how her last child was called Thomas.

The girl told me that she loved Pittenweem, because it's a fishing place, and because she used to visit her grandmother down there.

I had dinner, scampi and chips, in a pub, because I was still hungry. I am a traveller in a foreign place. I sit tranquilly among the chatter and laughter of the locals. It is not so foreign.

> In spring, some go to the park, and climb the terrace, but I alone am drifting, not knowing where I am, like a newborn babe before it learns to smile, I am alone, without a place to go.
>
> Tao Te Ching, Ch. 20

Chapter 24: A day at Markinch

It rained softly overnight. You could hear the soft trickle of water down the drainpipe. The leaves outside my window were glistening. But I thought it might be alright to go out. The weather app on the phone said not too much rain, but it might be windy.

I walked out to the road from the university campus and waited for a bus to Leuchars Station. It's about ten minutes' drive north of St Andrews: yes, north! There was a lady (American) at the bus stop who had her bags with her. She had been studying at the university. She was going to the airport (Edinburgh) by bus, and she told me to catch the X99 to get to Leuchars Station. I am going to Markinch.

Markinch is the town where Ellen Welch was born and grew up. Her father was the manager of the coalmine at Markinch, called Balgonie Furnace.

On the platform at Leuchars there were many passengers going on the London train, then in another fifteen minutes the train to Plymouth (my train) came. In the meantime, I bought a coffee from the little kiosk on the platform. It was only three stops to my destination: Cupar, Ladybank and Markinch.

The land was intensely farmed, meaning that all the land was in use. There were a few "casual" rural pursuits, like riding horses, but mostly it was crops and fields scattered with those huge circular bales that you could never lift by yourself.

I got to Markinch about 10 am. It was quiet. There was a carpark at the station, so there must be commuters who travel to work from here. I walked down the street and I saw only a few shops: a chemist, a hairdresser, etc, in among the street-front houses. I walked up towards a spire. I thought a church might be a good place to start. I had this idea about the coal-mine, and old photos, but some things are better done online, while some things are better done in person.

It was an old stone town with many cobblestones in the streets. I realised that perhaps in the 1960s, everyone tried to get modern, and they faced the stone on their houses with the same concrete-type covering: what we might call "pebblecrete" in Australia, that is used on driveways. I'm sure it gave everyone the impression that they were modern. After a few decades, though, the effect tends to be shabby and run-down.

The church was in front of me, up a steep rise, at the top of the hill, so it looked out on the town. When I got near the church, I saw a sandwich board in the road that said: "Tea and Coffee". I had not found a place for tea or coffee, and I was immediately persuaded.

I walked into a large community hall. It was on the left of the road; the church was on the right. A dozen ladies and gentlemen were sitting around a large table enjoying tea and scones. I was welcomed, and asked if I had come far. Apparently, the invitation to newcomers is always open. I said I was from Australia. It always seems redundant: people know as soon as I start to speak. And I consider my accent to be non-existent. It is neutral, not broad.

I shared my stories about some of the ancestors. I told part of the story of Ellen Welch. I said it was about 180 years since she left, and perhaps I am the first one in my family to come back here. I said she had done well in Australia in her marriage to William Archer, the convict. I suppose, in a church hall in rural Scotland, it may all sound shocking.

I felt like I was the prodigal son coming home again and telling the "good" stories. I didn't talk about Ellen getting pregnant and running away, never to meet her parents again. But I did find it awkward to tell Ellen's story, because it does raise questions: why did she leave, and why did she go alone when she was still so young?

It was a pleasant chat amongst everyone. One of the men then invited me to come over the road and have a look at the church, and also, come to the parish office to see the records they have. They have collated what information they could from the graves and the church's records, and it is in a pdf document on the church's website.

I was shown a file in a ring binder. Last night, I had written out the core family members whom I thought might be here: Ellen's parents and siblings, and her brothers' wives, and their dates of death. From the church's list, we found "Helen Forbes, next to Alexander's stone". So, this is Ellen's mother, and Alexander Forbes, her mother's father. There were several other members of the Welch family buried here, according to the burial records, but there is no gravestone. What they have is the records of burial.

The last burial in this cemetery was in 1854, which is the year Helen died. Her husband, Alexander Welch, died in 1860, and if he is anywhere, he would be in the new cemetery across the other side of town. I didn't feel up to that excursion.

Two of the men had written a book about the church in the early 2000s. It was a piecing-together of the history of the church, which went back to around 1000 AD. The first building was followed by another two buildings later on. My guide said some of the theories and assumptions they had when they wrote the book turned out later on to be mistaken, so the book would have to be written again. It is out of stock. They were keenly interested in how the church was constructed.

[*The Church In Markinch,* 2010, by Ian Gourlay and Ken Wilkie.]

I learned more aspects of masonry from this session. They had closely examined masons' marks. Every mason had his own mark, to say he was the one who had fashioned the stone, and there were also Master Mason's marks, to say the stones were approved to be used in the building. (At Durham in the Cathedral, a lady had said that the marks also indicated what money was owing to the mason, and you could see the marks high up on each pillar in the church.)

The men at Markinch had examined how stones were lifted too, using pulleys.

My guide took me into the church. The big excitement was that in 2009, an arch had been discovered and uncovered, that they did not know was there. It had been under plaster for perhaps two hundred years or more. The plaster was pared back and the arch was exposed. Then, a lady had painted a mural around it, and she did such a beautiful job that it looked like an extension of the arch.

The layout inside the church has changed over the years. There is a pulpit, as one would expect, but there is also a second storey of pews, so some people climb up the stairs to sit up there for the church service, including frail old ladies who have always done so. There is an organ that is much more recent; it dates from the 1930s. He said there is a boiler that heats up water that is used in the pipe organ. I had not heard of that concept. He said it sounds really good.

Upstairs on the right-hand side there is a set of pews for the Balfour family. The family is still important in the district. I saw a gravestone outside for a Balfour who was a Lieutenant-General in the British Army. The Balfours would come up their own staircase to their pew, and their servants would sit behind them. This occurred until quite recently.

The church has some items of furniture that come from other churches in the district that have closed down. They haven't decided what to do with them yet. So, the life of the church continues to evolve. It usually has services weekly. At the moment there is a pause because the minister has left and they are in the process of acquiring another one.

I walked around the church and the surrounding cemetery. I found one gravestone with the name Dryburgh, which might have some relevance, through Ellen Welch's father, Alexander: his mother was

135

Margaret Dryburgh. She died in 1820. [Later: No, the grave I found was Alexander Dryburgh, died 1831, aged 71, not in my records.]

I walked back through the town. There was no place for lunch, just a place for coffee and cakes, which did not interest me at the moment. There was another food place (or rather, a sign for a food place) which said it was online only, but also cash only. I couldn't make sense of that, so I passed it by.

I didn't think there was any point walking out of town to find the coal mine; I suspect there is nothing to see. The history books will have to address that. I walked back to the station and a train had just pulled into the platform. I was able to get on it. It was about 1:30 pm.

Without going outside, you may know the whole world. Without looking through the window, you may see the ways of heaven. The farther you go, the less you know.

Tao Te Ching, Ch. 47

I got off at Leuchars and waited ten minutes for a bus, along with about eight other people. Ten minutes back to town, then I went and found something to eat, at a place called The Country Kitchen, in a narrow alley. It was nice.

I walked down to see the ruined St Andrew's Castle again. At first glance it was disconcerting; it looked different to yesterday, but then I realised it was high tide now, and it had been low tide yesterday. I also walked past a wedding (on a Thursday), with men in kilts, a bride in white, an old church, and two fancy cars. One man in a kilt was watching over the cars. I had a closer look, and they were Aston-Martins.

The amusing thing about that was that the last time I went to the UK (in 2018), the people in the office where I worked festooned the walls of my office with puns on the name Martin, which included pictures of Aston Martins.

I return to my bookshops quest. I went into Waterstones a second time, with my head clearer, and there was just one book on the Tao Te Ching. I also went into Topping & Co, and found a few offerings. There was a book on the Tao Te Ching, and the following books on the I Ching: Stephen Karcher (*The Total I Ching*), John Minford's book. No, that was it, just two books. There was also Benjamin Hoffman's inspired book, *The Tao of Pooh*, plus a book on Confucius, and another book on Taoism.

Do any of these books sell in St Andrews? This town has lots of traditions they hold onto, so where is the room to explore something on the fringes? They have initiation rites at the university. Obviously, they still have weddings for young people (I have evidence). It doesn't leave much room for cultural and religious oddities like the I Ching.

Also in Toppings was a book called *The Book That Broke the World* by Mark Lawrence. (It is part of a two-volume saga.) Is this a plausible premise? And is that what the I Ching threatens to do: break the established institutions and the social fabric? I remember thinking that some people would have been offended by my book, *Future*, because it contains the idea that established churches do little good for people, and they hold them back from their own growth.

I looked at some reviews of Mark Lawrence's book. There are now three books: it is a trilogy: *The Book That Wouldn't Burn*, *The Book That Broke the World*, and *The Book That Held Her Heart*.

Could I write like that? Do I want to? [Later: I purchased the first of the books.]

The reviewers on the book-review website were the full spectrum from adulation to heavy criticism. I guess you have to be able to take that if you are an author.

I have finished reading my book: *The Silent Traveller in Edinburgh*, by Chiang Yee. It was nice to read that after I had just been there. Many things are the same now as in the 1940s. I like his Chinese perspective too. There is an easiness about his way of looking at life, as if he were always at peace, and his perceptions come out of that. I wonder if I am still wound up too tight, and always unhappy with myself or despondent.

Chapter 25: Cupar and the trail of the ancestors

Today I want to go to Cupar, by bus. It takes about an hour. It is overcast but not raining. I did not have dinner last night, because I did not want to go out. For the first time, I had breakfast at the dormitory, that is, a cooked breakfast. Every morning, I have had fruit salad and a cup of green tea. Today I also had scrambled eggs, mushrooms and tomato.

The bus left from the bus station, although I could have caught it on the nearby main road close to the dormitory. It is a 59 to Edinburgh. It stops at Cupar Rail Station. I arrived at 10:30 am. I found a Costa's Coffee place and had coffee and tea cake. Then I walked, wanting to go into the main road of the town.

I walked in the wrong direction. I made a mistake near the beginning (north is south, west is east). Although, I suspect I also just wanted to walk. The trouble was, after I had walked for half an hour, I was getting impatient to be where my "proper" destination was.

Not to worry. I had walked in a large circle, and I found myself next to a canal (the River Eden) and walked through a park. But again, I walked in the wrong direction. Part of the trouble was that I didn't see any road signs, but to be honest, I was still misreading Google Maps. After another thirty minutes, and I had seen much more of the town, I found Crossgate, which is the main street of the town. It is another old stone town. I needed number 33, but I couldn't find any numbers down the street.

I went into the library building, because I thought I could ask them (so, I could say, I have learned one new skill), and there was just a chance that the family history group was in the library. And indeed it was, upstairs. The building was very nice. I think it was built in the 1880s (I have photos) for the benefit of the poorer classes of people.

Upstairs I met the chairman of the Fife Family History Society. He asked me who I was looking for. Quick, to the point. I started off with the Welch family, then the Mackie family, and the Bridges-Richy marriage. I needed to get out my laptop, which I had brought, because I was getting mixed up between people. That was fine; the chairman was a calm gentleman.

I am noticing that lots of development happened after the Mackie family left: new buildings, changes in local government, changes in the churches. Some churches, for example, did not exist until after 1850, so I find myself thinking about what the towns looked like when they emigrated.

I explained to the chairman about the parish council's judgement on Robert Bridges and Margaret Richy, the rebuke, the disdain and the five-pound fine. My impression seems to be shared: the church was powerful, and it was severe. I think that as people became more educated, they were not so superstitious, or tolerant of the churches' presumptions. And also, people were leaving for other places, both in Britain and overseas, so the power of the church atrophied.

The library and the family history group closed for an hour for lunch. The chairman said he would follow up if I sent him an email with the documents about this episode. He also invited me to join the society, and I did.

I walked around for an hour. There is a Baptist church which is squarish and sideways rather than long. Next to it there is a Church of Scotland, which is grand but not overwhelming. Down the street there is a corn market in another grand building. The market was authorised by the king or the government(?), and it meant the local governing body could levy taxes as well.

Down the main street there are numerous closes, all very narrow and winding. They are all named.

I had lunch at a nice little café in a square. After that I went back to the library, because I wanted to send an email. I had to join the library. It was a temporary membership, for two weeks. Mission accomplished.

Afterwards, I thought there was probably a museum in town, and I looked up Google for an answer. There was, next to the rail station. It was two rooms, manned by two senior gentlemen. Its main feature was the history of curling in Cupar. It started in the 1700s, and it continues today, with international competitions. This mostly means Canada. One of the attendants had a friend who went to live in Australia, and he was a Curler. He went to New Zealand to participate in curliing competitions.

I lifted the object that you hurl (is it called a curl?). It is very heavy, about 20 kg. Women started to play it in the early 1900s.

There was some information about the railway line through Cupar. It started in the 1840s, so that was one of the things that was happening when the Mackies left. An interesting time to leave, although many Scots were emigrating with them.

I left the museum and waited for a bus. It was about fifteen minutes late, and there was another bus (the same number) close behind it. I guess it's hard to run everything on time. Life intervenes.

I got back to St Andrews; it's still overcast.

I went to the bar at the dormitory instead of going uptown. I had a drink and a chicken burger: an effortless accomplishment of dinner.

I had finished reading my book, so I put on my headphones and listened to music, the first time I have used the headphones, and the first time I have listened to music since I have been overseas, if I discount the children's singing in the church at Nottingham. I heard some old songs, and some new things I haven't heard before.

I have no plans for tomorrow, but it's my last full day in St Andrews. The traveller doesn't need to always have plans; the tourist does.

In the pursuit of learning, every day something is acquired.
In the pursuit of Tao, every day something is dropped.

Tao Te Ching, Ch. 48

Chapter 26: The offerings of Pittenweem

It is overcast but not raining. I am thinking of going to Pittenweem today. I think it has been overcast but not raining every day. I had to sort out my phone; The rental period ended the other day, and I had better have it available until I leave the UK in case I need it for messages. I went to the Vodaphone shop in St Andrews.

I had thought it best not to tackle this renewal on my own, and my experience confirmed my suspicion. It involved some counter-intuitive actions, like needing to have the UK sim in the phone, but then having to put the Australian sim in to complete the transaction. It only worked because the young man used his own phone to tether my phone and get a signal. Does that make sense? The phone had to be connected to make the renewal (UK version), but the transaction could not be completed unless I had my Australian connection, because my bank wanted to validate my presence for my credit card.

Enough to say that this took around forty minutes, an extraordinary amount of time for a simple thing. Next, I went to Tesco's to buy a packet of tea bags. Fortunately, I got back to the bus station in order to step straight onto a bus to Pittenweem.

The trip to Pittwenweem took about forty-five minutes. It was a double decker bus and I sat upstairs: a different perspective. I got more of a feel for the country. The wind was windy, and the fields were wild with movement, like a great sea in motion, weaving this way and that, but as smooth as anything.

If you were living in this part of the country, there would have still been a big chance that you worked on the land rather than being a fisherman. My impression of Alexander Mackie is that he did whatever came to hand: his father had been a seaman, and he had been a weaver, then a stonemason. I am thinking he had an appetite for life.

The bus driver let me off near the beginning of the town and I walked in towards the "town centre" and the harbour. There is a scattering of shops; it is not really a town centre. Later in the day, I noticed people travel to towns where there is an Aldi, and carry parcels of shopping back with them. I think Crail was one such spot, but not Pittenweem.

For a while I thought I might have to go without food until I got back to St Andrews, but it soon became evident that there were a couple of cafes, along with other essential services, like hairdressers! But my first foray was to the library. It is important to find a toilet at regular intervals, and I thought this would be a good spot.

The library was open, and outside there was a table of books for sale. I needed a light book that I could read on the plane, and I found one: *The Cornish Coast Murder*, written by John Bude (a Cornishman) in the 1930s. That sounded perfect. It cost me one pound, and I had the cash.

When I went in to pay for the book, I struck up a conversation with the two librarians about family history. There was also another woman listening in, not rushing in to get served. I had not thought of myself as a conversationalist before, but now it is easy for me to spin a yarn, like my great great grandfather, the weaver. I have a multitude of stories at my fingertips, and it all flows.

I talked about the Mackie family at Kilconquhar, and the librarian gave me the correct way to pronounce it; yes, I have heard numerous variations. "C'nnacker" is common. My claim is to be able to spell it correctly!

I walked down the street to a café, on what was a nice sunny day now. It was the kind of café I like: airy, not too small, and not a dominance of chocolate. When I walked inside, parked on my left was a very large pram with a brand-new baby in it. It was such a sight! The baby was peacefully asleep. The carriage was special, like one from a grand house 200 years ago, with large wheels, and leaf-springs. I stared at it.

After I sat down, another lady came into the café and wanted to talk to the mother, as she was very taken with the pram. The mother was well into her forties and the baby in the pram was her fourth child. She had had the same pram for all of her children. She said it hadn't caused a moment of trouble. It had been polished and oiled and kept in out of the weather. It sounded like a mechanic talking about a car he wanted to sell. What a funny story!

I walked down the steep slope and rocky stairs to the harbour. There was a row of houses along the shoreline, and maybe thirty fishing boats. They were kept in a tight little harbour, concreted in with steep sides, just like a fold for a flock of sheep.

The tide was on its way out. I walked out along the pier to the little lighthouse at the end. It was sunny but very windy. It almost blew me over. I wonder what it must be like on a stormy day! Across the Firth of Forth you can see the Edinburgh shoreline, and the island in the middle (the Isle of May).

In a little cottage at the end of the row of small houses there was a sign saying there is group meditation once a month, and refreshments afterwards. Climbing up again to the street, I noted the name 'Wynd' which is as common as 'Close'.

The journey of a thousand miles starts under one's feet.

Tao Te Ching, Ch. 64

Also on the way back up the hill, I stopped near a cave in the hillside. A man was on duty. This was the Cave of St Fillan. He lived in the cave around 700 AD. He is now the patron saint of mental illness. I had never heard of him. The man was looking after a video clip that was inside the cave. It showed a group of people playing a piece with violins and cellos. It was about seven minutes long; it was lovely. The man said that the music was their response to the hermit. The cave was about twenty metres long, and light came in from a shaft at the far end, so it looked sanctified.

A few other people came in to look. The man who was on duty had made the clip. He said he was not particularly religious, but he had an affinity for the cave and the hermit. I told him about my encounter with the hermit at Oatlands in Tasmania: the priest who was living there as a hermit, and who talked to me for an hour and a half. (I wrote about it in *Travel with a Pen*.)

From a website: "Think for a minute about where the village of Pittenweem got its name from and you might realise that 'weem' is an adaptation of the Gaelic 'uamh', meaning cave. Pittenweem actually means *place of the cave*, and indeed there's a sizeable subterranean chamber under the hillside off Cove Wynd, the alley connecting the village harbour to its High Street. This chamber is St Fillan's Cave, a natural cavern probably carved by an underground river thousands of years ago. The miracle-working Saint Fillan is believed to have lived in the cave in the 7th century, reading and writing in the gloom with the help of a luminous left arm. Inside, you can visit the stone altar, explore a dead-end passage and see the steep steps creating a former entrance to the cave from above. The cave is still a minor pilgrimage site, with Christian services occasionally held under the rock roof."

My comment: doesn't the name "weem" also sound like "womb"? And it is not too far from the sound "Aum".

I was up the hill from the hermit's cave, at the church (Church of Scotland), which had a cemetery, so I went in to see who they had interred there. You can get the story of a whole town in the cemetery: which families were the leading families, whether dying at sea was important, what other occupations people had, how many children died, if there were any military in the town, and what money and finesse people invested in gravestones and monuments.

After an hour, I didn't find much of apparent relevance to my family. There may have been some peripheral connections, but I don't think there were any pivotal people. No Mackie, Garvie, or Hood. There is another cemetery too, but it is a "New Cemetery", which I think is after about 1870.

The church was solid and square. I don't know how old it is. It was locked.

I walked around some more. This was a small place; I was unlikely to get lost. There was an art gallery on one corner of a street. I went in. There was a lady sitting there reading (in the sun; the sun was coming in through the windows). The gallery didn't look very presentable. There was a sign saying there was another gallery down the street, and this place was just showing off one artist's pieces. But most of the pictures were stacked against tables and walls, not positioned for showing.

No matter. I had a chat with the lady. She had worked in Vietnam for six years, and for three years in Qatar. She had been a student at St Andrews long ago. I chatted too, about where I have been and what I do now: write books.

I went back down to the harbour. I had missed something: there is a new monument, a statue of a woman and a child, to represent people who have lost someone at sea. It was lovely, in bronze: the child was about six years old. The mother looked sad but brave. There was wisdom and longing in her faraway look.

I walked back up to the main street and found the bus stop. The bus came in two minutes. It was a saga of a trip, because the bus driver kept having trouble with the ticket machine, and the bus must have stood alongside the road for ten minutes while he fiddled with it; quite extraordinary. There were lots of people getting on and off the bus too.

I had not had lunch, and I was thirsty. When I got back to St Andrews, I walked down the street and went into a pub, and had a beer. I thought I would get food later. I wandered aimlessly, into Market Street, which I may have seen before. What I saw this time was that it had a second-hand book shop, called The Bouquiniste. I went in.

It was a small shop. And I found an I Ching book that I do not have: Henry Wei. I had heard of the book, and I have thought it would be good to obtain. So, a very pleasing find, for 7.50 pounds.

While I was doing this, an American lass was debating with herself whether to buy seven volumes of Virgil in good condition. She was a translator at a university in the USA, and this was a good find for her. I recommended that she commit the indulgence, buy them, and post them home. I told her I had done the same, and the expense was well worth it. Neither she nor I is the person that will spend a thousand dollars on golf clubs or Disneyland, and one does not commit such indulgences very often, so one is advised to do it. She will value those books for a long time.

[Later: At home, I am reading a book by a book dealer: Rick Gekoski, *Guarded by Dragons*. He would have made sense of the two of us.]

I brought my Henry Wei book home and then went out for dinner. I thought Indian for the last night would be appropriate, and it was very nice, except that I ordered too much food. There was a young couple next to me, and the girl was making nonsense talk, likening the guy to a Chinese animal (rat, horse etc), something which probably didn't even make sense in her own head; it constituted a mere conceit.

The guy didn't have a clue what she was talking about and was a bit embarrassed, or felt that there might be grounds for embarrassment. I thought his only grounds for embarrassment was in being seen participating in the conversation. (Then I think, it is not necessary to be so scathing.) They left after a while.

The next couple were an older Scottish couple. The man looked like my neighbour from when I lived in Horseshoe Creek, Kyogle; he was a maker of high-class period-reproduction furniture. This couple were having one of those serious but routine discussions that some married couples have, about business affairs they were each involved in. It was serious, but it did not ruffle the substance of their relationship. I found it admirable.

I walked home. I went to bed around 10:30 pm, when it was finally getting dark. All was quiet, as one might expect. Then, a few minutes later, a series of explosions started, as if they were about half a kilometre away. My immediate thought was of some boisterous student prank or activity; I think I am probably right. The sound was not quite like fireworks going off, but it wasn't like the neighbourhood blowing up either.

The episode ended about five minutes later with a much larger bang. I have no explanation; it smacked of student mischief, or what one calls shenanigans. There was no evidence the next day of a calamity having occurred.

There is so much of life that one never knows.

Chapter 27: Edinburgh Castle

It is light at 4.00 am. This is the morning I leave St Andrews. I got up and had breakfast in the common room. There is a bus to Edinburgh at 11:20 am. The journey takes just under two hours. I walked up to the bus station. I thought it would take me thirty minutes, but I made it in fifteen (I know my way), so I was in time for the earlier bus.

When I think back to my arrival in St Andrews, in the night-time, the route I took today was not the route indicated by my phone that first night. Why would this be? My route today was through the grounds of the university, through a car park, and along a roadway to the bus station. It was the most direct route, and all of it was through public lands, nothing private or obscure. Does it mean that the technology is currently not such that it can be universally depended on? If this is the case, how would one know the occasions on which one should not trust it?

And there is a huge underlying psychological factor as well. When something goes wrong, my immediate instinct is to blame myself. I am sure I represent fifty percent of people. (The other fifty percent immediately blame someone or something else.) And of course, we are all wanting to be competent, not useless. A lost traveller is a sad tale of incompetence, or perhaps misadventure.

Onwards, onwards, this is your path.

Siddhartha, Herman Hesse

The first bus changed at Glenrothie, where we got onto a fancier bus for the rest of the journey. We arrived in Edinburgh about 12:30 pm: very civilised. We drove over the high bridge over the Firth of Forth. It still strikes me as impressive.

Fortunately, there was a toilet at the bus station, and also the small café, so I could get something simple to eat. This is about the sunniest day there has been. I walked up to St Andrews Square and sat in the sun for a while. I have started my new book: *The Cornish Coast Murder*. It's a genteel murder/detective story. I remember a few years ago at a book fair I found a hardcover book that was about different types of detective stories. It was a compilation of stories from well-known authors; I think Dorothy Sayers was the principal editor, and she wrote the introduction. [Later: The book was *Great Short Stories of Detection, Mystery and Horror, Part 1: Detection and Mystery*, and indeed it was edited by Dorothy L. Sayers. It was first published in 1928. My edition was from June 1950, a month after I was born.]

I walked slowly down to St Leonard's Street where the Airbnb is located. It took me the best part of an hour, but I walked slowly. Then I found a coffee shop to sit in and have coffee and cake until it was the right time. Tom met me at the door. It is a four-storey building. Fortunately, I am on the first floor, not the top floor. It is an old building. Everything seems to be done on the sly for Airbnb; Tom said to say I was visiting a friend if I was asked.

Tom told me I am the first person to occupy the flat. I noticed there was a washing machine in the kitchen, so I said I was interested in that. He said he would go and get some detergent. There is no wifi, but I can probably use my phone to connect, given that I have got a month's supply of data.

The most amazing thing about the flat (apart from how far out of town it is!) is that it has a direct view of Arthur's Seat. It is directly opposite the lounge room window (Arthur's Seat was mentioned in *The Silent Traveller in Edinburgh*). Those huge crags of rocks are sitting right in front of me.

Tom came back with the washing detergent, and I washed my clothes without mishap. He also bought a rack on which I can hang the damp clothes. This experience with the front-loading washing machine was positive, unlike my experience at Waterford, where all the clothes came out sodden and took two days to dry. I am not blaming the machine; it was that there are many things I simply do not know about. I have an upright washing machine at home. I know how to use that. My problem is that it is assumed that I know how to operate these unfamiliar things.

After I had done my washing, and spent some time reading my murder book, I went out for dinner. I walked for fifteen minutes, and I found a Vietnamese place that was quick and simple. It's still strange to me that it does not get dark until 10:30 pm.

The next day: Today I have a tour booked at Edinburgh Castle at 1:45 pm. Until then I have time.

I checked last night, and at the Vietnamese Restaurant I had been close to a post office, so I went back there. I had two tasks; one was to change some money from Euros into British pounds, because I only had five British pounds left, and I had 150 Euros. The second task was to post more books home. It's expensive, but it's nice not carrying the extra weight. Also, when I was in Vietnam about fifteen years ago, my suitcase was overweight, and that was expensive too.

The post office opens at 10:00 am, not 9:00 am. A few people were waiting. At first glance, I thought the staff were going to be bossy and rude, but after observing them for a while, I realised they were just enjoying their job. It wasn't rudeness; it was gusto, or relish. They use Textas to write on the front of letters and packages, and pen on the back. I put my Edinburgh address, but he wanted the postcode as well. I said I don't know that. It got ignored. The parcel cost about 35 pounds. Oh well.

I thought it would be good to go to an art gallery in my spare time. I went to the National Gallery, which featured art from the 1700s to modern times. In Scotland, people have particular ideas about what Scotland is. The themes here were about cities taking over the countryside, and the importance of continuing to appreciate nature. And there were portraits of children, and groups of people. And important people, and royalty. And Edinburgh. And Sir Walter Scott: the man, his novels, his importance to Scotland.

[Later: I went to the Knox Grammar Book Fair when I got home; it was a couple of weeks after I returned. I found (and bought) a novel by Walter Scott: *Old Mortality*, first published in 1816. It was one of his earlier novels. The book was hardback, dark blue, small (11 x 16 cm), and it did not have a date of printing on it.]

One of the themes I pondered was why my ancestors left, or what they felt about leaving, and what they missed about Scotland. All the great themes are contrived. For example, even though down the street there are men playing bagpipes, it's a tourist attraction. They didn't feature in any of the art. In fact, nor did any music. You could argue, then, that the art is not representative, or that music is not important. But I don't think that; I think they are like different rooms of the same house.

The scenery of Scotland was clearly important: the dramatic nature of mountains and rivers and forests. I also wondered about how difficult it was to move around in the 1800s, just to go from Fife to Liverpool so one could emigrate would have been quite an effort (it's around 280 miles).

I bought some sushi for lunch, to eat in the park; always a good meal.

I am (mostly) able to move around without getting lost now. That's a bold statement. Just to prove it, I found my way to the Writers' Museum and sat in the courtyard for a while. I didn't go into the museum again. I remember this, however: among Robert Louis Stevenson's memorabilia was a sheet of paper with the plot of *Treasure Island* on it, written by Stevenson as a ten-year-old child. (He wrote the novel when he was about thirty.) People's views about writers are interesting; so are writers' views about writers. For some, it's as if what they do is a holy thing. For some, it seems to be an exalted thing in relation to people in other occupations in society.

The trouble is, what writers write could be ordinary, trivial or forgettable, or many things worse, or regrettable. What makes a writer exceptional? Is writing esteemed just because it has been successful, that is, popular? Think of how people have talked about the British-made "Downton Abbey" as something above the ordinary. (was that in Bath? No, that was the "Bridgerton" series.)

[Later: The big house in "Downton Abbey" was Highclere Castle in Hampshire. The village scenes were at Bampton, which is a few miles west of Oxford. It was the "Bridgerton" series of which I heard a tour guide in Bath say: "It was filmed here."]

I walked up the hill to Edinburgh Castle. I had my ticket on my phone, and there was a time attached to it, but it wasn't clear to me what one was supposed to do. I milled about with other people. There was a place where you could pick up an audio headset, but I didn't do that; I find that it cuts me off from my surroundings. I had purchased the guidebook, so I thought I would read about it afterwards.

I walked up the hill. There are three or four different areas on the way up. There is an area with cannons. You can also walk up along the wall and look through arrow emplacements. It is so far down below to the town, but you can see it all, especially to the north, to the Firth of Forth. There are areas up the top for military, such as the Dragoons. There is also a war memorial building, which has books with lists of Scottish soldiers who served. There is a square where people were lining up to see the Crown Jewels.

There was one massive cannon (six tonnes) with 20-inch cannon balls, which was built in the late 1700s as the weapon to end all weapons. It beat some enemies into submission by sheer intimidation. It had a name: "Mons Meg".

There were lots of small tourist groups with a guide, many speaking in foreign languages. This is probably the most crowded place in Edinburgh. I bought my ticket two weeks ago, and I saw a sign on the way up today saying it was sold out today. There is a tea-room at the top, and also a whisky-tasting place.

Travel used to be a pleasure, now it has become an industry.
Travel seems to have become a lost art.

Lin Yutang, *The Importance of Living*, New York, 1937

I wondered about the Robert Louis Stevenson novel, *St Ives*, and I remembered there were prisoners at Edinburgh Castle in the novel. Apparently, it has always been used to keep prisoners, even up to the second world war, and back to the 1500s. There was an exhibition section fitted out as the prison, say, around the time of the wars against Napoleon. There were a couple of doors with carvings on them that prisoners had done, and relics of their confinement here. I got the impression that Stevenson's novels were accurate.

I bought no souvenirs. I have no personal interest, and when I think about all the people that I could potentially buy for, there are around fifteen, so it is just not going to happen.

I walked back to the apartment. It took about thirty minutes, but I did not get lost. I did not get lost! I stopped in at an Oxfam bookshop and perused their wares, but I did not buy a thing.

I found some food in the fridge, so I do not have to go out and buy dinner. I am reading some more of the Cornwall novel.

Tomorrow night is the Sarah Blasko concert. It's only about fifteen minutes' walk from here. Also, I checked out how to get to a new place on Wednesday, so that I will be close to the airport. There is a bus nearby that goes to the place I booked. It will take about forty minutes. I think I will have to get a taxi to the airport on the final morning.

Chapter 28: Coalmining in the Scottish Archives

By 7:30 am, already the sky has given me blue, cloudy and overcast. Across the road is a line of four-storey buildings, all with regular stacks of chimneys in banks of eight in a row. I don't know why the chimneys in Edinburgh are designed this way, but they all are. And on the first stack, yesterday morning, on the right-hand side chimney, a seagull was sitting. This morning it is not there, but the seagulls are wheeling about

Last night I finished the book I was reading: *The Cornish Coast Murder*. It was enjoyable. You could also call it sumptuous storytelling. John Bude fed the story out to the last drop. As well as the detective aspect, there was also the social milieu that it presented: the vicar's associates in a small rural town: very settled, nothing disruptive or controversial occurring, apart from the occasional harassment, rape and murder.

I do have one more book I haven't read: *Philosophy of the Home*, that I found in the Topping bookshop here in Edinburgh.

It did look as if it might rain today, so I thought I should do something inside a building. However, my thinking was waylaid when I walked around the corner (or you might say, it was immediately fulfilled), because a building there was called the National Archive of Scotland. I was curious, so I went in. I was thinking in particular about the history of coalmining at Markinch, or Balgonie Furnace,

The man at reception thought I might be lucky, so I went upstairs. I put my quandary to the librarian, and before you know it, she had introduced me to several websites with resources about the history of coalmining in Britain. She also brought me several books on the subject. It was good to get a context for coalmining, so I can see how Alexander Welch fitted into it, and what kind of man he might, in general, be.

Some of the books I skimmed for the history of coalmining, which went back to around 1000 AD when monks used to use coal for warmth. They did not sell it. The methods for obtaining it were crude. Also, towards the Middle Ages, the coal that was used most

155

was what was accessible from the seashore. The reason was that transport of heavy things was difficult, due to the roads being rudimentary, whereas you could put a boat right up close to the shore and load it from there.

The period of most interest to me, 1820 to 1860, came before the nationalisation of coal. Nationalisation and Maggie Thatcher came as two emblems of the termination of the coal age in Britain. One of the books was about changes in management and technology in the 1800s. I think this is an important perspective. I asked the librarian if she would copy me out the whole chapter that was about mining and management. The author said most mining managers were lousy, because it takes quite a wide range of skills and understanding to manage all of the things that are required of a manager.

Also, another librarian came over to me and showed me maps of Markinch and surrounds. This was remarkable, because I had only looked at such maps just before I left home, so they were fresh in my mind. But he showed me how to use the different kinds of maps for each place, and maps from different periods of time, to get a much more nuanced view.

That was a fruitful morning. Then I walked down towards town. I had morning tea. I could have got a sandwich, but they didn't seem to be organised to provide a vegetarian sandwich, so I had cake!

I found my way to Blackwell's because I wanted to look for another book to read on the plane. I was also aware that I could look in one or more of the many second-hand bookshops. I looked in various sections, including the Scottish fiction and non-fiction sections, but I did not walk out with a book.

I arrived at the Royal Mile, which is a long slow descent from Edinburgh Castle to the waterline. I started walking down it. I think I have got some clues about the geography of the town: I should be able to turn right at some point and find my way back to St Leonard's Street.

However, I found a place to explore first: The Scottish Storytelling Centre, which is also a museum about John Knox. The odd thing about this was that I had tried to find the Storytelling Centre the other day, but it was not there at all, at the place where the map said it should be. I am sure I was not wrong about this. Moreover, having found the centre by accident, it looked as if it had been on this site for a long time. It had not moved here recently.

The irony is that this building is one of the oldest buildings in Edinburgh (1500s) and it is said to be the oldest existing building that has been used as a shop. This building is also famous for the time that John Knox spent here. It is in the older part of the building, while the storytelling centre is a new building patched onto it.

I went through the museum, the part about John Knox. He was a reformer in the church who wanted to rid the church of corruption. Mary was the Queen and she was wedded to Roman Catholicism. Knox wanted to be done with the Roman Catholic church (it was just before the time of Oliver Cromwell) and it was the time when John Calvin was alive. Knox lived in Italy for a time: so his perspective was very much influenced by European ideas. I don't remember all the history, but it is quite clear that Knox was prepared to part Queen Mary from her head.

Beliefs were important to the people of this time, worth killing for.

There are three levels in the building, with several small rooms, and it is structurally much the same as it used to be. I took my time. There were some exhibits of books, prayer books and histories of Scotland. John Knox was a prolific writer.

One could view John Knox as heroic or as abominable. One could view him as a necessary link in the chain from the past to the present. I think it is probably best to refrain from judging the past. The tough questions for us are: what am I prepared to do in the present? What is worth fighting for? What is worth killing for? And what would I never do? And what would persuade me to shift my perspective from one to the other? And what would I be prepared to lose (including my own life)?

One could take up one of these positions and still be lost.
The answer is not in the map; it is not even in the compass.

There was a bookshop as part of the Storytelling Centre, with a few books about John Knox, and books about stories. I bought a book about stories. It was geared towards children, but also to the idea of the role of stories in the lives of all people. The author, Jenny Moon, had taught storytelling to teachers at university. Do I have any of her books? I might. The book I bought is called *Folk Tales of Rock and Stone*. [Later, after a slow search of my bookshelves: I don't think so.]

I also picked up a booklet advertising a month-long event coming up in August. It's called Fringe 2025: thirty-two events with traditional and contemporary storytelling, and music, theatre and spoken word. I will miss it. If I had been here, would I have attended? Possibly. Would I have belonged? Possibly not.

After a cup of tea, I went on my way down the hill. The traffic was now at a standstill in both directions. People just seemed to accept it. I went past a witches' shop, so I went in and asked if they had any I Ching books. The lady knew what I was talking about, and she thought they might have had one or more books, but she established that they didn't have any at the moment. The shop was called The Wyrd Shop, Canongate.

I'm not thinking to pursue this any further. I have sufficient threads to weave. I am still pondering what the answer is to my question: is the I Ching fading away today?

I kept walking down the street, and eventually I saw that it went to Holyrood, the Royal Precinct. The Scottish Parliament is opposite. It

seems that there is something on at the palace today, and that's why the traffic was disrupted. It is also why I saw so many people dressed up in their finery in the middle of the day. They were walking down to see the King, or something like it.

I heard bagpipes, and there were men standing on parade inside the grounds. There were policemen guarding the gates. I stopped for a few minutes, but there was nothing here that I desired to see. I walked back to my flat. I am getting reasonably good at navigation now. But, man's true delight arises from the contemplation of mystery....

Chapter 29: Sarah Blasko in Edinburgh

It is overcast this morning. There is the faintest whiff of cloud above Arthur's Seat. I have to leave this morning to move to a place closer to the airport for my flight tomorrow morning: Silverknowes.

Last night I walked downtown to see Sarah Blasko at The Cave. It was just past Blackwell's bookstore: turn right and walk down a close and then walk back up the street. There is a sign above the doorway that says, "Let he who has no mathematics not pass through here." I am not sure what prompted the sign, but I pass: I used to teach mathematics.

[Later: I discovered that it is a variation of the sign that was purportedly inscribed above the entrance to Plato's academy, "Let no one ignorant of geometry enter here."]

I did read some history of this building. It goes right back to the early days of Edinburgh. It was a merchant's store for a long time. I didn't read that it was ever an academy.

The faintly perturbing thought that lies behind the saying, however, is that someone who can't read maps should not enter here, particularly if you take the Platonic version of the saying: ignorance of geometry.

The building was disused and forgotten until about twenty-five years ago, when it was rediscovered. Now it is a venue for music functions (with seating for just sixty-five people!), and weddings and other private functions.

The Caves makes up the sub-structure of the 18th Century South Bridge. The website says, "Every room has a story to tell and a special place in Scottish history, from vaults that served as the stables to the French Cavalry who were at one time bodyguards to the Royal Family, to remains of the houses that pre-date the Bridge itself."

There was a bar in the venue, but no food. That was fine; it's been good to be less dependent on three meals a day. I talked to the people at the bar about my travels and my family history discoveries.

The people at the bar didn't really know Sarah Blasko. She was booked by the people who book these things. There is a support act called Slow Leaves. It is one man: Grant Davidson, from Winnipeg, Canada. I don't understand the economics of these events. Sarah was playing with three musicians. Surely no one would get paid very much.

I liked Grant: his music was nice, and he was interesting. I bought his CD. I didn't buy anything of Sarah's, because I already own it all. The house was full, bearing in mind there were only seats for about sixty people. Most people seemed to be locals. I met one Australian man who has been living in Edinburgh for the last few years because he is married to a Scottish woman.

Grant played one number with Sarah. She played her latest album ("I Just Need to Conquer This Mountain") all the way through, then did some older numbers. I didn't remember much of her new album.

Much of it, I suppose, I had only heard once, at The Factory at Marrickville in Sydney. I have not been listening to music at home lately.

I spoke to Sarah after the show. I don't usually do this, but there were not many people present, so there was an opportunity. I told her I had listened to her since she started: twenty years ago. I had seen her at the Woodford Folk Festival in Queensland in December 2004. I said she had developed a great body of work, and I hoped she would keep working on it. She said she appreciated that.

I walked home. It was about 10:30 pm, a fine, cool night. Summer in Edinburgh. Apparently, it is raining torrentially in Sydney and on the central coast.

It's been a good trip. There have been plenty of satisfying things happen. I will go home and work, although it is not clear in my mind what that means. I don't know what I want to create, but I want to be a little bit clearer about it, not just let it dribble out aimlessly. It was interesting listening to Sarah Blasko and Grant Davidson talk last night about what they do and what they think about the writing and performing process.

The real voyage of discovery consists not in seeking new landscapes but in having new eyes.

Marcel Proust

There is an objective perspective and a subjective one. What does that mean? I remember the storytelling centre, and I wonder if talking about story all the time just becomes self-referential drivel. The very thing that a story is not is an account of something real. It is a fireside yarn, made up. People get emotional at a war memorial because it is something that really happened, not just something made up.

161

I can't deny that people want the made-up stories; they are a part of life. But what is the difference between them and something grounded in reality, history? I suspect that some people would regard my distinctions as crude or mistaken. Yet for me, my question still stands.

For the first time recently, the overcast morning did become a drizzly, wet day. I moved out and walked over to the next street (Clerk Street) and waited at the bus stop, trying not to get too wet. I was waiting for the 37 bus to Silverknowes. It was a long ride through the city and out to the northwest, the region of outer development, flat and featureless. I went right to the end. It was about 11 am, and check-in at the new place was 3 pm. I hadn't thought this through.

I talked to the bus driver. I thought I would be best to go back to the city and find somewhere to be for a few hours. I ended up going with him: the 16 to Torphin. However, as the bus was going on its way, I realised it was coming into Newhaven. This is the harbour, and I had intended on visiting it. It was also mentioned in *The Silent Traveller in Edinburgh*. So I got off there.

It was still wet, and I had the heavy suitcase and the backpack. I was at a harbour. There was a rectangular dock with a dozen boats moored in it (it was low tide). At the opening (yes, it was just like a sheep fold), there was a small lighthouse. Out in the bay there was a small cruise ship (200-300 people rather than the ones with 3,000 passengers that you see regularly in Sydney Harbour). There was a fish market to my right along with a couple of restaurants, and a hotel in front at the end of the walkway. I walked out to the hotel and stood around for a while. People were coming off the cruise ship and getting onto half a dozen buses. Life goes on for the tourist, even in the rain.

I would have liked to have explored, but I would have got saturated. I talked to a group of tourist information people, who were obviously there to tend to the cruise-ship folk. I realised they were not government tourist information people. But they were happy to chat; it was a wet day. There is a local walk you can do, that is tagged with QR codes. On a sunny day it would be enjoyable.

I went into a big restaurant and had a coffee while I thought about what to do. The coffee was nice. After a while I decided to have lunch there; it seemed to be a good place to try fish. I ordered a fish curry, given that there were a few Indians working here, and I thought that boded well. However, it was awful, utterly tasteless. Maybe it doesn't matter when you have boatloads of tourists ordering food, who will never come back again. I found it disappointing.

> The first kind of false travel is travel to improve one's mind. The second kind of false travel is travel for conversation, in order that one may talk about it afterwards. The tourists are so busy with their cameras that they have no time to look at the places themselves. This sort of foolish travel necessarily produces the third type of false travellers, who travel by schedule.
>
> Lin Yutang, *The Importance of Living*, 1937

It was still drizzling. I waited for a while longer in the restaurant, then I simply waited at the bus stop; at least it was a shelter. I left Newhaven at about 2:15 pm so I would get to Silverknowes about 3 pm.

I arrived. From the bus stop it was supposed to be about ten minutes' walk to the place I had booked. And I half a notion that I might be reasonably competent now at navigation. But the route was confusing. I realised that all the streets were named Silverknowes! It was only the suffix that differed: Close, Road, Bank, Hill, Crescent etc. Amusing, but not really. Anyway, I did figure the route out eventually and I arrived. It took me about thirty minutes, but no matter.

Then there was the next challenge. I had no instructions, just the door in front of me. There were two doorbells. What does one do? I rang both of them. That produced no response, so I knocked on the door. That also got no answer. Not to be stuck in this position, I looked for a phone number on my phone, and rang it. A man answered. He sounded "distant", but I stated my case. I am at the door. I wish to enter.

The man said he was in Miami. I was surprised, but I didn't care. He had taken my money happily enough when I made the booking. He had to deliver right now. He gave me a code for a keylock next to the door. I managed to open it. That gave me access to the key for the door. I still needed to find a room inside.

The man on the phone wasn't helping much, but I heard a person inside the house. A young man came to the door. The man on the phone wanted me to give the phone to the young man in front of me, which I did, but the man in front of me got annoyed with the man on the phone, and hung up on him. So, there was a dose of humour in my situation.

I was shown my room upstairs. It was a windowless bedroom with a small bathroom to the right of the entrance. Fortunately, this was just a bed for the night, and I would be leaving in the morning quite early.

The bedroom was full of a family's personal things: books, family photos on the walls. I was in a family's personal space. Later, I looked more closely at the photos. Three or four of them were baby photos, and not just baby photos, but photos of babies on the day they were born! Rather personal, and not for public showing.

Then the young man showed me a kitchen area downstairs. You walked through a windowless lounge room with a gigantic television screen in it. Then you came into a kitchen and dining room. The kitchen was really long, with two fridges. At the end of the room was a doorway into a laundry. There were piles of laundry lying around. The backyard was claustrophobic, with suburban clutter: barbecues, cubby houses, privacy screens, clotheslines.

In the dining room there were lots of books, probably sixty metres of shelf space, but it was all popular (pulp?) fiction. I made a cup of tea and read a chapter of my new book. Then I retreated to "my" room. I leave early in the morning for the airport. The bedroom has cupboards which have no doors, but which have curtains draped across them. They are full of people's clothes.

The rain stopped and the sun came out: a nice afternoon. I managed to order a taxi for tomorrow morning. Everything is so difficult, things that used to be simple tasks. Once upon a time, you would ring someone up, tell them what you wanted, and get them to commit to do the job. Human-to-human interaction and commitment. All this is gone. Instead, I try to type it out on the computer, and still it seems simple, just a few minutes.

But then it goes astray. The computer rejects something I've typed. Not only that, it throws the whole process off course, and I find myself back at the beginning, and I don't know why. And I don't know if the system has recorded what I just did, or some of what I just did, so that when I go back in, it will tell me that I've already done that or, there is already a user with that account.

After three times of this, I realise I have already spent fifteen minutes on it and I am nowhere. That's when I wondered if the phone would actually work better. But I know, I am still going to be in combat with AI. I rang a phone line which was for booking taxis. I gave it my name, phone number and email. Then my time of pickup (tomorrow morning, and my address. But it says goodbye, somewhat peremptorily, and I discover that I have a message on my Gmail.

The message says that I have a taxi booked for tomorrow morning. This is good. And the pickup address is correct; this is also good. But there is a destination, and the destination is the same as the pickup address. I don't know when that happened. You can imagine a human having a good laugh about that one, then fixing it. But there is no such corrective for AI.

Perhaps the taxi driver will arrive in the morning and refuse to take me anywhere, because the destination is the same as the embarkation point! We live in an age that is quickly becoming mind-numbingly dysfunctional. It is not okay.

After the ordeal, I went for a walk in the sunshine. I discovered you can walk down to the "beach". The suburb of Silverknowes has a waterfront on the Firth of Forth. You can't quite see the bridges that go over to Fife, but you can see the shore of Fife. Where the bus stopped this morning there is a golf-course, and you can walk down the rise to the waterline.

I learn history. The suburb was previously part of the Lauriston Estate. This used to be all farmland. Most of it was sold off in the 1930s to build housing. However, the rump of a farm remains.

There were people walking along the sand of the "beach" and among the rocks, mostly with dogs. There was a promenade, and people were walking along that, and jogging along it. There is a kiosk selling ice creams (called Mackies!) and the like, but it was closed; too late now.

Parked along the road were about ten campervans, just like I saw in New Zealand in several places. They know how to find each other and congregate. Maybe there's a website for grey nomads.

Further along the waterway I saw the small cruise ship I saw at Newhaven this morning. It confirms that I am looking at the same stretch of water. So, I have completed some forays today.

On the way back, I didn't see any places where I could get a meal. Best to let it go. My host said I could cook in the kitchen, but I will leave cooking until when I get home. It hasn't done me any harm missing out on a meal here and there.

> A true traveller is always a vagabond. A good traveller is one who does not know where he is going to, and a perfect traveller does not know where he came from. He does not even know his own name.
>
> *The Importance of Living*, Lin Yutang, 1937

Chapter 30: Long journey back to Sydney

My taxi booking worked. He was there before 5:30 am and I was on time too; I was packed up and ready. I thought the airport was close, but it took around thirty minutes to get there. I confessed my ineptitude with the booking, but he said many people make mistakes with the booking system, and he figured I was probably wanting to go to the airport.

(Of course, he may have just been saying that to make me feel better. And I thought, thanks for saying that anyway, and once again, am I too old to travel now? Not because I am frail, but because it is often so difficult communicating with the prevailing technology. Things are worse, in so many ways, not better. But I am not supposed to say that, because then I would be a whingeing old man. And so, we cultivate blindness all the time.)

Then it was into the awful rituals of airports, and the not-knowing what to do from moment to moment. What is happening now? Who knows?

But I managed to board the flight to Doha around 8 am. I was in seat 30D, the first seat in the middle section (3 + 3 + 3 seating), and there was no one sitting next to me, a small luxury. We got to Doha about 5 pm. I don't know what the weather was like. In the air, one has no vision of the outside world; one is completely cut off. We all live in a yellow submarine.

I found some vegan food to eat at the airport, which I think is better for when travelling. It was tasty and satisfying.

I found the place where we were to board the next flight, all the way to Sydney, so I was sitting there, waiting patiently, and this happened. There were dozens of people sitting around, and amid it all, there was a boy, only about six years old. He had a small suitcase, a solid one that he was sitting on. It had a handle and some wheels, but it also had a front end that looked like a scooter.

But then, he pulled the front up, sat on the suitcase, and pressed a button. It immediately became an electric scooter-thing, gliding forward. He rode in wide, lazy arcs around the concourse, like he was naturally the coolest young dude in the world. He did that for twenty minutes, then went back to sit with his family. A lady was sitting near me with her boyfriend, and when she saw the small boy on his scooter, she cried out spontaneously, "I want one of those!" and I said, spontaneously, in response: "Yes, we all do. We all want one of those!"

Another observation: a young lady was sitting opposite me, and she was typing on her laptop. What was she typing? She typed for over thirty minutes, calmly. Was it part of a great novel she had just begun? Was it the outline for the great novel she was going to write (like Robert Louis Stevenson when he was ten)? Or was it a set of observations that would later be incorporated into her first great novel?

Or was it practical: plans for her proposed revolutionary business?

When I got on the new flight, I was seated between two young people: a man and a woman. The man lived in Wollongong; he had just been in England, Scotland and The Netherlands for two months as an engineer. He works on sleep apnoea products. We talked.

The young woman was Malaysian, but her family went to live in Edinburgh when she was a young child. She had grown up there. She was going to visit an Australian person she knows in Brisbane.

Another interesting thing happened during the night (I think it was night-time). When the young woman settled down to go to sleep, she brought out a teddy bear and held him. The bear was small, a bit less than a foot high (30 cm). This was the second bear I had encountered on the trip.

The bear looked quite self-possessed, as bears usually do. I wanted to ask the young woman questions about the bear, because bears have turned up a lot for me in the last few months: enough for me to start writing articles about them and their relationship with humans. But in this case: Who is the bear? Where did he come from? What is it about the bear that makes him a worthy companion?

Then there are the harder questions: is it not embarrassing to be holding a bear while you are going to sleep when you are twenty-plus years old? (Obviously it is not.) What place does the bear have in this world, for you? But I didn't ask those questions, and in the morning (or whatever time it was that the airline thought we should wake up), the bear was stowed away again.

I had been given a teddy bear (whom I named Edward Bear) when I was six. He was similarly self-possessed, looking at me with those steady eyes, both dispassionately and compassionately, as if he knew everything about me but he did not judge. (Of course, this description is my adult self reflecting back on myself as a child.) Looking back, I think he was the first "person" to make me aware of myself, and want me to make the best of myself.

This flight was very full. It felt cramped. The blinds were drawn for most of the journey, even during the day, so it felt strange; once again, as if we were in a submarine. The journey is about fourteen hours from Doha. Just before we arrived in Sydney, I realised it is now Friday. I had believed that the day of my return was Thursday, and I had told my son that. I don't know what went wrong. I did read "Thursday" on the original message I received about the flight.

The plane arrived about an hour late as well. Getting through to pick up my suitcase was the usual trial: there were about a million suitcases, and was mine among them? Maybe! Fortunately, people are usually forbearing with each other. I guess they bear in mind that everyone has had a long flight, over twenty-four hours in all. My suitcase did eventually turn up, looking quite familiar, and unlike the million others, many of which were huge.

I realised that when you are out and about in a foreign city, you never see the huge suitcases, only the smaller ones. The people with huge suitcases must go straight to their fancy hotels and stay there.

Getting through the security process was as mystifying as ever. I put my passport on a machine, and then it said, "Take your ticket". What ticket? I hadn't realised that the apparatus had printed out a ticket that I was supposed to take with me. And why? In the next queue, I had to hand this ticket to a man, along with the Incoming Passenger Card I had filled in on the plane.

Then we had to go to Queue 6. But jubilation! Queue 6 was the exit to the external world! No interrogation, no intrusive inspections!

I found a Vodaphone booth, and the young man kindly replaced my UK sim card with my Australian one. I rang my son, and he told me of his tribulations last night, when he tried to pick me up but I was not there. Finally he rang Qatar Airlines and gave them the flight number. They told him it wasn't coming in until Friday night.

So, I have lost track of a day, even though it all seemed seamless enough, and there doesn't seem to be any room for argument with a digital world clock.

I found the train station and travelled to Central, then changed to the metro to Castle Hill. At Castle Hill I looked for a taxicab and one found me while I was walking down the street. He found me! This is the opposite of being lost, I suppose. I was home by eight o'clock (pm).

I don't want to start thinking about too many things. I am tired and it's time to settle. I heated up the dinner that my son had cooked for me last night. Salmon and vegetables; that was very nice (and much better than the tasteless fish curry at Newhaven the other day).

I have written over 50,000 words. To what end? The end (to be trite).

It is good to have an end to journey toward; but it is the journey that matters, in the end.

The Left Hand of Darkness, Ursula K. Le Guin

A quote from Westminster Abbey: "Thou art the journey and the journey's end." This was for Micheal Mayne, who was the Dean from 1986 to 1996.

Epilogue, Part 1

I had arrived home; time to think about what it meant, because there are two sides to us: we are the journey, but we are also the journey's end. I did not go on this trip in order to have things to tell people, as Lin Yutang said, or pictures to show them. Nor did I want to take a trip on a rigid schedule, where you have allocated the amount of hours for each of the sights.

And yet, it is difficult to go travelling unless one has some kind of structure. This is the conundrum. One needs to buy a ticket before commencing, and probably several tickets, or else it will simply not be possible at all. How does one plan without creating the kind of strictures that Lin Yutang is suggesting?

It is not as if we are all oblivious to this conundrum. We know it, which is to say, we know there is a tension between rigid planning and chaos or, alternatively, aimlessness. Accordingly, we know there is an appropriate point of balance, a sweet spot between the two extremes. Our problem is to be able to recognise where that point is, and to attain it.

But, in pondering this dilemma, one may note the statement of Marcel Proust: "The real voyage of discovery consists not in seeking new landscapes but in having new eyes." And how does one acquire "new eyes"? What effort is needed to change this aspect of ourselves? We can't focus on that. We can say, today I will go and see Stonehenge, or climb to the top of Arthur's Seat, but I can't say, today I will see with new eyes.

Another of Lin Yutang's statements is also problematic: "A true traveller is always a vagabond. A good traveller is one who does not know where he is going to, and a perfect traveller does not know where he came from." There may be truth in what he says, but it is also true that the person who has no plan for the day, and nothing to hope for or attain, often does not even get out of bed. I have always found it is better to get out of bed in the morning.

One's goals need not be grand, or apparently impossible, although, I know some people like it that way: "Today I want to achieve impossible things!" But no, I do not find that approach helpful or even attractive. It is not for me. I would rather be a vagabond. However, I would want to be a vagabond like Siddhartha in Herman Hesse's novel, in his later life beside the river: "As time went on, his smile began to resemble the ferryman's, was almost equally radiant, almost equally full of happiness, equally lighting up through a thousand little wrinkles".

So, I think the conundrum is actually this: if one wants to be happy, one must already be happy. Ultimately there is just light, radiating everywhere. One does not go travelling because one wishes for experiences that will make one happier, or more fulfilled, or that give you a platform for broadcasting your experiences to others. When you are at one with the Tao, the Tao welcomes you.

However, one lives in the world. We have to accept the constraints and implications of that, taking them on, not as a burden, simply as the conditions of living. I had six weeks in Britain and Ireland; I gave myself no more. My funds had a limit which, I suppose, I set myself. My goals were mostly shaped around questions in family history. I also had to address what the need was to be in the various places when so much is now available online. What was I going to learn in Fife that I didn't already know from family history websites?

At this point, my goals started to look intangible or gratuitous. I thought it might be helpful, illuminating, just to be in the places my family had left, even though it was so long ago.

I was going to places where my ancestors had come from. One day they had packed their bags and left, for whatever the reasons were, and never (as far as I can tell) came back. It is very possible that most of the emigrants never even had any contact with the family back in their homeland, ever again. And here I was, I felt, 170 or 180 years later, turning up again.

I think of walking into the church hall at Markinch and being faced with twelve people sitting around a table, saying to me, "Who are you? Where did you come from?", to which the obvious answers were: "Glenn Martin. Australia." But the answer was so much more. My great great grandmother left here around 1840, alone. She went to Sydney, Australia. She married a convict from England, and they had eight children. He ran a hotel in Sydney called the Duke of Edinburgh.

So, yes, ultimately we are simply light radiating. But we have to start with our circumstances and see what we can do, in the flesh. I look at these great great grandparents with admiration, even awe. In the church hall, I felt that I was bringing back a message from Ellen; she was from this town. Her family was from here. She sends you greetings. All is well. She made a good life in Australia.

I think of the theme of lostness. I certainly did not plan that. But I have to think about what I felt when I became aware that I was lost, and what I felt on all the different occasions when I had the realisation that I was lost. Some of it I could simply blame on my ineptitude with the phone and Google Maps: in a broad sense, with technology. And also with the decrepitude that comes with age: my poorer eyesight, my problem with the glare on the screen of the phone.

But I do not subscribe to the truism that decrepitude comes with age. An old tree puts forth new shoots. Even the broken bones of old people heal. I am alive; I am continually regenerating. My experiences of lostness cannot be simply attributed to age or ineptitude with technology (although, the frequent perversity of technology has to bear some blame!).

It is said that we learn the lessons we need to learn, or the experiences will keep coming to us over and over until we do. But I think of what Gayle Forman said: "Traveling is not something you're good at. It's something you do. Like breathing." We are surrounded by trite sayings, but what Gayle is suggesting is that being lost may not be something that can be dismissed as simply a lesson we need to learn. It may in fact be an ongoing condition. It implies, at most, that we can get better at learning how not to get lost. It doesn't mean that we will never be lost again.

There was that moment in South London when I was as lost as could be. I had walked for one or two hours, and I thought that it was only a matter of time before I came to Herne Hill Station. (What could go wrong?) It was on a train line! Surely that would become obvious sooner or later. But was I heading in the right direction? Had I turned myself around and lost any sense of north-south, east and west?

There was a moment when I felt paralysed. I could not take a single step forward anymore, nor a single step back. Not one step, in any direction. What was I to do then? I just stood there. More than anything, I was disappointed in myself, the failure to have any innate sense of direction. My years as a Boy Scout, walking in the bush for whole weekends and coming back home safely. All gone, to no avail.

You could say this was an old conceit. You could say I was cavalier with the planning of my journey back to my lodgings. You could say it is easy to get lost in the city ("I feel lost in the city", Jon Anderson). I could argue that I was no worse than many people; many people get lost in the city. My expectations of myself were unrealistic. Or you could say I just needed to get better at the learning process itself. Get the paper map out again, spread it out on the floor, and review all the steps of your minor disaster. Where were you? Find the points on the map and imprint it in your mind.

But we seldom do that, do we? But I also ask, was there something positive about what I was doing? Well, I was out there, "having a go".

175

I was pushing myself a little bit more than I had before. I was becoming more confident about getting on and off buses and trains. This was all true, and all good. Perhaps the real problem was my feelings, the feeling of paralysis.

As it was, someone turned up. The lady with the child in the baby buggy said, "Are you okay? Can I help you?" Some people believe there are angels that are always close to us, and they show up to help when we really need it. Her willingness to help was quite disarming. She walked me to where I needed to be, so I was found again, but more than that, she talked constantly, about anything, and pulled me out of my disappointment with myself. She offered lightness.

I don't say she was an angel. And there was the moment in the park where she stopped and sat down to have a cigarette. It's hard to imagine an angel stopping in order to have a puff on a cigarette. Yet I keep the door open for the unusual, and I welcome acts of kindness. I like to be independent, but the lesson, if there is a lesson, is that sometimes, you need a bit of help. You can't do it on your own.

In the midst of my lostness, I just had to relax. The writer Richard Rudd says, "Relaxed, you will naturally draw support from others, and you will not resist help. At the astral level we are connected to other people, always."

There was that epic day, my first day in Ireland, when I was helped by about a dozen people to get to my destination. I think of those words of Pico Iyer: "We travel, initially, to lose ourselves." As if this were the very point. And I think of the plaintive words of Martin Martin (1655-1719), visiting Glasgow from his home on the island of Hirta: "When he walked through the streets, he desired to have someone lead him by the hand."

This seemed an extreme thing for an adult to say, but then I looked at Hirta on the map. It is way out in the ocean, west of Scotland, all by itself, although it is part of the St Kilda archipelago. In the 18th century there were 180 residents. The island was evacuated in 1930, when the population was down to thirty-six residents. Visitors can go to the island at certain times of the year only. Although his surname is Martin, he is unlikely to be a relative of mine, and I cannot claim to be overwhelmed by the size and complexity of cities. I have lived in them for a long time.

I suppose I could claim to have had sufficient commitment to get me to my destination that day. I could have given up earlier in the day and stayed in Dublin, but I was intent on getting to my destination. I was not stuck or expecting the path to be unproblematic. I persevered, taking the next step at each point.

Was this maintaining my faith in the outcome? Some people say the beginning of a project is critical, because your commitment to the project creates the energy that will bring the project to its fulfilment. It is more important than competencies. It lessens obstacles, and it presents you with solutions when you are facing an obstacle. I thought the last part of my journey to the apartment in Waterford was unbelievably wonderful.

I am close to what I think is the door to the apartment, having come all the way from Bath today, and it being after sundown, and I can't send a message to the host. What can I do? Do I give up and go down the street and get a room in the hotel (if there is a room)? And there is a man right there who is willing to help. And there is a lady who offers to connect to my phone with her wifi, and she can't because she can't figure out the password, but then her daughter arrives, and she knows about the password, so I am connected. In minutes, I am in my room.

I found this whole chain of events extraordinary. I was left feeling great gratitude to all these people. Later, I found this statement by a Chinese writer, Hua-Ching Ni, that seemed pertinent: "Life is movement, and movement cannot be stopped. One should neither fear to move nor lose the stillness within." The movement was, I think, my unwavering commitment to my journey, even to the point where it could have been regarded as folly.

I am not taking credit for my commitment. It was more like, I simply kept moving. Getting to the apartment in Waterford was simply what my goal was for the day. Accordingly, there was no question of giving up, despite my hovering on the brink of rational defeat more than once*. (*"Rational defeat" is when there is simply no way possible; for example, if you do not have wings, you will not be able to fly. Wanting to fly will make no difference.)

You could say, I was in danger but I was not drowned.

My time in Waterford was also subject to its own influences. I thought I had come here to find out more about Sarah Crosby, my Irish great great grandmother. But then, several times, I found myself telling her story to people, until I thought: perhaps that is the point, not to find out more, but to tell what I know. It was the same as in Markinch. I am coming back, after about 170 years, and I am talking to Irish people about one of their ancestors, who was also my ancestor.

It was most notable when I went to the Irish Wake Museum. They talked about death rituals in Ireland. That was when I thought I should share what Sarah had designed for her funeral, in 1897. She had it written into her will. She wanted all of her grandchildren to have good clothes for the funeral. In the family tree, I counted up how many there were, and there were fifteen. I asked the guides what they thought of that, as a provision in a will.

I had told them some of Sarah's previous story, as the girl who had been shut out of the Refuge for the Homeless in London, and who had stabbed the policeman in the arm when he had her pinned down on the ground with his knee in her chest.

They thought it was a story worthy to be told. One of them said Sarah may have been remembering something from a funeral she had attended in her own childhood, so her act was either recreating an event where something happened that she admired immensely, or it was her response to something that had taken place back then that was regrettable. So, we both learned something new. They learned about the episode, and I learned a new way of looking at the episode.

"Onwards, onwards, this is your path." (Siddhartha)

Epilogue, Part 2

There was the occasion when I was lost in a meadow outside Oxford, and a girl came to help me – twice. The first time, she said, "You are going the wrong way." Blunt, but not harsh or supercilious. The second time, she said, "You are going the wrong way again. I saw you from over there, and I thought I had better rescue you. You're in my debt now." She was young, younger than all of my children, and she was reversing the roles. I was the student that had failed, one more time, and she was the teacher, gently but firmly putting me back on the road towards competence (and performance of an elementary skill or task).

And yet she wasn't. Rather, she was play-acting the role of teacher. In the face of my inexplicable ineptitude, she was giving me the gift of dignity, and I was acknowledging this. I said that was okay, to be in her debt. Being lost repeatedly was certainly an affront to my dignity, and she could see that, and met it with kindness. I think that later that day, talking to one of her friends, she told the story, not with amusement, but with bemusement.

Was it a trial, one of the trials which life presents to us, and we must face? Was it part of the great journey which makes us a better person? It was a small thing, and no lives were at stake. I have to ask, what was the problem? Why didn't I go the right way the first time? Or the second? What was misleading me?

My glib response is that I hadn't been around Oxford for about 180 years, and at that time, I was only two years old when I left. (This was Edwin Eaglestone, my great grandfather, in 1859, leaving Bletchington with his parents to go to New Zealand, and then Geelong.) But, of course, that is merely a joke, because (mostly) we don't remember anything from former lives. So, was it a deep lack of confidence in my ability to map the terrain, or was it the opposite: taking the issue of identifying the terrain too lightly?

However, I have to acknowledge that later, I walked back from town to my flat the same way, without getting lost. I went through the park, I crossed the little footbridge, I walked along the track through the fields and took the turn to the right at the correct place (not going straight ahead) and entered the street where the flat was. Perhaps my concern about getting lost has overshadowed my successes or, more importantly, my ability to learn the layout.

The words remain: "You are going the wrong way again." But now I think about what the encounter taught me. I observe that getting lost the first time could be attributed to my difficulties with technology, but the second time was not.

There was a question that applied to the time after I came home. Had I learned some new skills of navigation through my troubles? You could say, how would I know, because I am probably only walking on familiar paths? But there was one occasion, a month after I returned, when I went to meet a friend for lunch, and the café was somewhere I had not been before.

I found the destination on my phone and I asked it for directions. I was back in my familiar southern hemisphere, so I could not blame the world for turning north and south upside down. And I did it again: I went in exactly the opposite direction to what I was supposed to. It was an agonising time; it took me twenty minutes to go in a big circle and finally identify where the café was, instead of taking five minutes. It was acutely embarrassing.

I could still blame the technology, but I think on this occasion that would be churlish. And obviously, the important thing is to get the start right. How do I work out which way I should be facing? It has to be about knowing where north is. What I need is a compass. As it happens, my phone has a compass. New rule: when I am walking to an unfamiliar place, I should take a moment to determine where north is, before I consult the map on the phone.

Was all my turmoil simply about an elementary technological skill? I think not. I think there were a number of factors, like the quizzical nature of Edinburgh's closes. But I think what I had to face was the idea that "strange lands are the traveller's lot". And I like what Lillian Smith said: "I soon realized that no journey carries one far unless, as it extends into the world around us, it goes an equal distance into the world within."

I ask myself, is that too glib? But I think not.

Behind it, I think there is the idea that we should be able to sense it, the right way to go. We should know it, deep down. And it was not as if I were Blaxland, Lawson and Wentworth trying to find a way over the Blue Mountains in 1813. Hardly. I was just trying to find my way to a destination which one could point to on a map, in districts where the streets had long been established.

Sometimes, I thought, "Just let me do it again. I'm sure I can do it this time." In Bath, I struggled to find the Royal Crescent, and after that, I struggled to find the Jane Austen Centre. If you look at a map, it doesn't look so hard. But, to be honest, my dedication to getting to a given destination contended with my curiosity. Yes, I know the Royal Crescent is further along this road, but the street on the right seems very interesting, and surely if I turn left later on, it will all be okay?

I did see a lot of Bath. If I recounted my important destinations, it would not seem as great as my feeling for the many streets I walked along, all the sights I saw, all the inconsequential things. I suppose that feeling lost sharpened my senses, too. But I am aware that there are always two versions of this. The first is being aimless. When one is aimless, it doesn't really matter which way you go. (Alice in Wonderland asks the Cheshire Cat which way to go, and the Cat replies, "It depends a good deal on where you want to get to," and when Alice says she doesn't care where, the Cat says, "Then it doesn't matter which way you go.")

Or, one travels, even when not sure where one is, with a sense of purpose, as if it all matters, and as if what one is seeing is absorbing, because one can absorb all that is there, the present, the past, the many pasts, and the longing for a good future. One finds oneself losing old opinions and default beliefs. You are small but your heart is becoming larger.

It was said of Francis Greenway (the ex-convict turned architect), who designed many fine buildings in Sydney and New South Wales in the time of Governor Lachlan Macquarie, that he had "absorbed the atmosphere" of Bath. That is not only true of architects. We are all here to "absorb the atmosphere".

You must overcome the inertia of all humanity and all of its past, to be present as one who can see the whole, and each small part (lost though one may be) as part of the whole. One is gathering various odd forms of energy and needs to master them. It is like domesticating small animals.

Epilogue, Part 3

My previous book had three epilogues. It made sense at the time, but I wasn't about to make it a habit. You would think an epilogue should be an epilogue: one only. And yet, I thought I had finished this book at Epilogue Part 2, but another question raised its head: if the true essence of a traveller is to be a vagabond, did I miss the point on my trip?

I was firmly anchored in plans. In testimony, when I came home, I worked solidly for a couple of months and was able to finalise a book, which contained nine stories of family history. Most of the stories had been finished prior to my trip, but a couple of the stories I figured out while I was away. You could say they "came together" through my experiences on the trip. It wasn't that I discovered startling new facts that provided the final clues to what happened in those stories; it was that the experiences gave me the necessary insights.

Thinking of Lin Yutang, who decried the fact that travel has become an industry in modern life, was I too tied to my family history outcomes to truly appreciate the unplanned and unexpected in my travelling experiences? Did I ever change course? Could I be accused of being a slave to a schedule?

I offer an analogy. In eating a meal, it is not good to be in so much of a hurry that one gets indigestion. Also, one does not enjoy the meal; one is merely swallowing the food as necessary fuel. But, one does not need to take all day to eat the meal. If one relaxes and enjoys it, the meal will still get eaten, and one can be on one's way. All in good time. This is a metaphor, but note, there were times when I did not eat, because it would have got in the way of something I wanted to achieve for that day.

To the best of my awareness, I enjoyed my experiences. I could say, sufficiently, but the phrase is best left unqualified. Or, I could say, fully.

I remember the man who called out to me on Leith Walk in Edinburgh one afternoon, who told me, "You look mint." It was a surprising thing for a stranger to say, but I took it as an affirmation of my ability to enjoy a meal, even if I was not going to spend all day eating it. There were other things to do (which I would also enjoy).

I don't think I missed the point of my trip. If I wished to be harsh, I would say, no one has permission to tell me that I missed the point. I made the point myself. It is myself that I have to ask: did you fulfil the point of your trip? And I say, it was satisfactory, most satisfactory. It was satisfying. If I had been travelling as a young person, my goals and expectations would have been different. If I had been a scholar of architecture, my plans would have been different. If I had been a rich person travelling, I might have been disappointed at times. But for me, the whole thing was a treat, as well bringing its accomplishments.

To understand why I set the goals that I did, one would need to understand what I have gained from searching into the lives of my ancestors. Otherwise, why would I have spent the whole morning of a rainy day in Edinburgh in the library of the National Archives of Scotland, exploring the history of coalmining in Scotland? What did I gain from that?

It was about trying to understand the experience of a girl of sixteen in Markinch in 1840, who was the daughter of the manager of the coalmine, who had found herself pregnant. Why did she make the decisions she did, so that she ended up in a remote cottage in the Hunter Valley in New South Wales, and married a convict? I think that she lived a worthwhile and enjoyable life, but how had she got there?

I return to Australia, to my home, to my library, and I think, the blessings of the ancestors be upon us.

Selected Bibliography

Thomas Cleary, 1986, *The Taoist I Ching*, Shambhala, Boston MA.

Herman Hesse, 1922, *Siddhartha*, Picador (1973), London.

Hua-Ching Ni, 1983, *I Ching: The book of changes and the unchanging truth*, Seven Star Communications, Santa Monica, CA.

Stephen Karcher, 2003, *Total I Ching: Myths for change*, Time Warner, London.

Lao Tzu, 1972, *Tao Te Ching*, trans. Gia-Fu Feng and Jane English, Vintage, New York.

Lin Yutang, 1937, *The Importance of Living*, William Heinemann (1946), Melbourne.

Margaret J. Pearson, 2011, *The Original I Ching*, Tuttle, Rutland Vermont.

Richard Rudd, 2009, *Gene Keys: Unlocking the higher purpose in your DNA*, Watkins, London.

Richard Wilhelm, 1950, *The I Ching or Book of Changes*, trans. by Richard Wilhelm into German, rendered into English by Cary Baynes, Routledge & Kegan Paul (1975), London.

"The Handbook of Lu, the Wanderer" is from the collection of poems by Glenn Martin, *I in the Stream*, 2017, G.P. Martin Publishing.

Acknowledgments

Thank you to the many people who greeted me and helped me along the way on my travels to Britain and Ireland in 2025. And thank you to all the volunteers and employees who helped me at the various institutions I visited.

And I give thanks to all the ancestors who trod the paths before me.

Author profile

Glenn Martin is the author of over twenty-five books. He is an independent scholar, researcher and writer. He has written books on ethics and values, the "bigger picture", family history, reflections on experience, and he has released several volumes of poetry. His career includes teaching in high schools, tertiary institutions and adult education programs. He has managed organisations in the community sector, written commentary on employment law, management and training for professional publications, edited a national magazine for trainers, and designed online education courses. His current work is to write books.

Glenn lives in Sydney. He lived for twenty years in a valley in far north New South Wales, where he wrote two books of local history. He has five children and four grandchildren.

Other books by Glenn Martin

Stories/Reflections on experience

The Ten Thousand Things (2010)
Sustenance (2011)
To the Bush and Back to Business (2012)
The Big Story Falls Apart (2014)
The Quilt Approach: A Tasmanian Patchwork (2020)
Long Time Approaching: An Incomplete Memoir (2023)
Travel with a Pen (2023)
Library Meets Book Fair (2024)

Books on the bigger picture

Future: The Spiritual Story of Humanity (2020)
A Singular Book of Great Esteem: Life with the I Ching (2025)

Books on ethics and values

Human Values and Ethics in the Workplace (2010)
The Little Book of Ethics: A Human Values Approach (2011)
The Concise Book of Ethics (2012)
A Foundation for Living Ethically (2020)

Books on family history

A Modest Quest (2017)
The Search for Edward Lewis (2018)
They Went to Australia (2019)
No Gold in Melbourne: A Scottish Family in Australia (2021)
All the Rivers Come Together: Tracing Family (2022)
The Sailor, the Baron and the Dressmaker (2024)
Ordinary People, Remarkable Lives (2025)

Poetry collections

Flames in the Open (2007)
Love and Armour (2007)

Volume 4: I in the Stream (2017)
Volume 3: That Was Then: The Early Poems Project (2019)
The Way Is Open (2020)

Local history

Places in the Bush: A History of Kyogle Shire (1988)
The Kyogle Public School Centenary Book (1995)

www.ingramcontent.com/pod-product-compliance
Lightning Source LLC
Chambersburg PA
CBHW022129080426
42734CB00006B/285